OSPREY
MILITARY

CLASSIC BATTLES

VICKSBURG 1863

GENERAL GRANT AT THE FRONT

RECORDER ART SUPPLEMENT, APRIL 24TH, 1892.

CONSULTANT EDITOR: DAVID G. CHANDLER

OSPREY MILITARY

CLASSIC BATTLES

THE MILITARY BOOK CLUB

VICKSBURG 1863

GRANT CLEARS THE MISSISSIPPI

ALAN HANKINSON

◀ *General Ulysses S. Grant, architect and executor of the Vicksburg campaign. This impression of Grant on campaign, and rather more carefully dressed than usual, was drawn by Schabelitz for the* **Recorder Art Supplement** *of April 1892.*

Key to Map Symbols

Army	xxxx ⊠	Brigade	x ⊠	Infantry	⊠
Corps	xxx ⊠	Regiment	iii ⊠	Cavalry	◨
Division	xx ⊠	Battalion	ii ⊠	Artillery	⊡

First published in Great Britain in 1993 by OSPREY, an imprint of Reed International Books Ltd. Michelin House, 81 Fulham Road, London SW3 6RB and Auckland, Melbourne, Singapore and Toronto.

ISBN 1-85532-353-2

Produced by DAG Publications Ltd. for Osprey Publishing Ltd.
Color bird's eye view illustrations by Cilla Eurich.
Cartography by Micromap.
Wargaming Vicksburg by Paul Stevenson.
Wargames Consultant Duncan Macfarlane.
Mono camerawork by M&E Reproductions, North Fambridge, Essex.
Printed in Hong Kong.

Illustrations on the following pages are reproduced by courtesy of the Anne S. K. Brown Military Collection: 2, 12, 13, 20, 21, 23, 26, 28, 34–5, 38, 41, 43, 49, 51, 52–3, 56, 60, 61, 64, 66–7, 68, 69, 74–5, 76–7 (top), 80, 81, 82.

▲ *Top: During the siege of Vicksburg, a mine was exploded under one of the Confederate forts, on the Jackson road. In the foreground of this contemporary artist's impression, looking remarkably casual, are Generals Logan and McPherson. Below: in the saps between the White House and the Vicksburg crater, 2 July.*

CONTENTS

The Western Theater of Operations, Autumn 1862

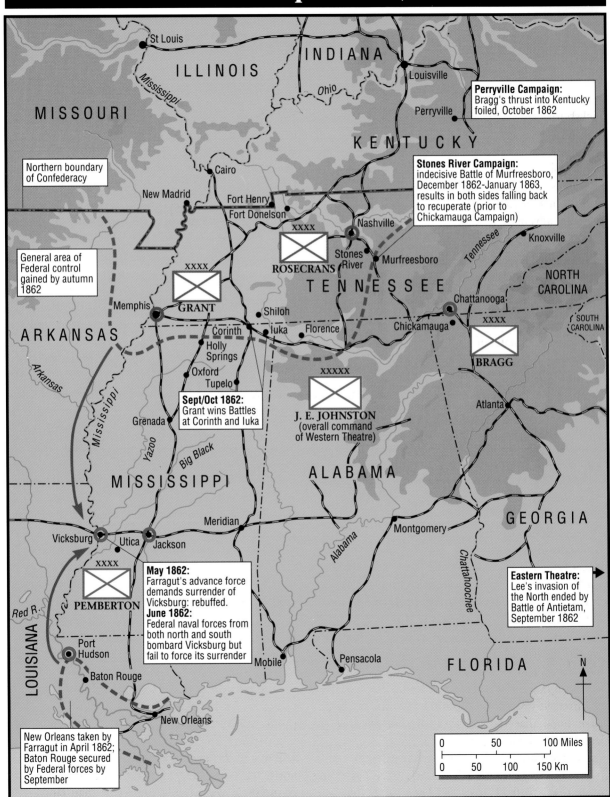

Perryville Campaign: Bragg's thrust into Kentucky foiled, October 1862

Stones River Campaign: indecisive Battle of Murfreesboro, December 1862-January 1863, results in both sides falling back to recuperate (prior to Chickamauga Campaign)

Northern boundary of Confederacy

General area of Federal control gained by autumn 1862

XXXX
ROSECRANS

XXXX
GRANT

XXXXX
J. E. JOHNSTON (overall command of Western Theatre)

XXXX
BRAGG

Sept/Oct 1862: Grant wins Battles at Corinth and Iuka

Eastern Theatre: Lee's invasion of the North ended by Battle of Antietam, September 1862

XXXX
PEMBERTON

May 1862: Farragut's advance force demands surrender of Vicksburg: rebuffed.
June 1862: Federal naval forces from both north and south bombard Vicksburg but fail to force its surrender

New Orleans taken by Farragut in April 1862; Baton Rouge secured by Federal forces by September

ILLINOIS

INDIANA

MISSOURI

KENTUCKY

St Louis

Louisville

Perryville

Cairo

New Madrid

Fort Henry
Fort Donelson

Nashville
Knoxville

Stones River
Murfreesboro

TENNESSEE

Chattanooga

NORTH CAROLINA

Memphis

Shiloh

Iuka   Florence

Chickamauga

SOUTH CAROLINA

ARKANSAS

Corinth
Holly Springs
Oxford
Tupelo

Grenada

Atlanta

MISSISSIPPI

ALABAMA

GEORGIA

Meridian

Montgomery

Vicksburg   Utica   Jackson

Red R.

Port Hudson

Baton Rouge

Mobile   Pensacola

FLORIDA

LOUISIANA

New Orleans

N

0		50		100 Miles
0	50	100	150 Km	

INTRODUCTION

Vicksburg was a long campaign, lasting some nine months altogether. It involved many kinds of warfare – a great deal of marching to and fro, much devising and revising of plans, massive works of engineering on roads and bridges and waterways, a bold amphibious operation on the Mississippi, a rapid fighting advance of dash and brilliance, several pitched battles, and a final, relentless siege. Throughout, it was the rebels, the Southern Confederates, who were defending; the Northern Federals who were on the attack, deep in enemy territory. There was considerable bloodshed and much wasted effort and, from the Northern point of view, there were many moments of disappointment and setback. But when the victory came at last, it was crucial to the course of the American Civil War.

It is strange to recall that two years earlier, at the start of the war, President Lincoln's chief military adviser, the veteran Lieutenant General Winfield Scott, had said that they should ignore the popular clamor for a march on the Confederate capital, Richmond, Virginia, and plan instead to move down the valley of the Mississippi, to gain control of the great river from its source to the sea. In this way, he argued, three of the rebel states – Arkansas, Louisiana and Texas – would be cut off from the others, and the naval blockade of the Confederacy would become complete. It was called the "Anaconda Plan," in reference to the South American snake that kills its victims by squeezing them to death. In the summer of 1861 the old general's advice was ignored and soon after that he was replaced. For many long, bloody and profitless months the main Northern effort was concentrated on the eastern sector, directed toward the capture of Richmond, in the naïve hope that the taking of their capital would destroy the rebels' will to fight on.

By the close of 1862, however, many leading men in the north, political and military, were beginning to see that Winfield Scott had been right, that con-trol of the whole length of the Mississippi would open the way to ultimate victory. The great obstacle lay in the rebel guns on the Vicksburg bluffs. President Lincoln in Washington, who knew the river well from his youthful days as a flatboatman, had no doubts: "Vicksburg is the key," he said. "The war can never be brought to a close until the key is in our pocket."

In the South, too, the importance of Vicksburg was fully appreciated. It was known there as "the Gibraltar of the Confederacy." In December 1862 President Jefferson Davis left Richmond to visit the threatened Mississippi valley and see what could be done to protect it from the invaders.

The city of Vicksburg stands on, and high above, the east bank of the Mississippi River, some 300 miles, as the river flows, north of the point where it reaches the Gulf of Mexico. The river is wide and powerful here, and the city is built on steeply rising bluffs and on the summit plateau 200 feet above the river bank.

The city derives its name from a Methodist minister, the Reverend Newit Vick, who purchased more than a thousand acres of land in the early years of the 19th century and began to develop the town. The place was already a thriving trading post, sending steamboats laden with cotton up and down the river. By 1825 Vicksburg had its name and the status of a city. The cotton trade flourished and before long it was an important commercial center, mainly dependent on river traffic but also linked to the east by the Southern Rail Road of Mississippi. By the 1860s Vicksburg was the largest city in the state.

Its commanding position above the river and the nature of its surrounding terrain made it a tricky proposition for an invading force, especially one approaching from the north. A direct attack by river was out of the question, and for many miles to the north, and spreading out both east and west, the countryside was often more water than land – the

Mississippi and Yazoo Rivers and the streams that fed them together with a bewildering maze of shallow lakes and marshy inlets, much land that was sometimes dry but frequently flooded, all of it overgrown with trees and shrubs, an untamed, watery wilderness. Any army wishing to take Vicksburg from the north had either to force a way, laboriously, through these obstacles or make a detour march of hundreds of miles across hostile territory to the east and north – or find some other, unexpected solution to the problem. This was the situation that faced Major General Ulysses S. Grant at the end of October 1862 when he was given command of the Northern Army of the Tennessee.

◄ *William Tecumseh Sherman was Grant's greatest fan and most trusted divisional commander. He thought Grant's plan for the march on Vicksburg was overbold and dangerous, but was the first to admit he had been wrong. Later in the Civil War he brought the lessons learned at Vicksburg savagely to bear on the "Deep South" from Atlanta to the sea.*

THE OPPOSING COMMANDERS

Grant is the central, key figure in the Vicksburg campaign. It was he who made the running. He was on the attack and, although many of his plans were frustrated and several advances turned into withdrawals, the initiative was his throughout. The Confederates could only react to his moves and try to guess his intentions, hoping for the best. But even when they got it right and Grant's attacks were repulsed, he promptly responded with new pressures and threats from so many directions that, in the latter stages of the campaign, the Southern commanders – John C. Pemberton and Joseph E. Johnston – were separated from each other and confused, unable to coordinate any effective action. Long before Vicksburg fell, its fate had begun to seem inevitable. Ulysses S. Grant fought many campaigns and battles during the Civil War, most of them with skill and success, but Vicksburg is his masterpiece.

He was proud of his New England ancestry – one grandfather had fought the British at Bunker Hill in the War of Independence – but had grown up in the rural midwest, his father being a successful farmer and leather manufacturer in Georgetown, Ohio. Such schooling as Ulysses received was basic and he showed little interest, preferring to help around the farm, especially with the horses. In the summer of 1839, at the age of 17, he was sent to the military academy at West Point.

This was very much against his inclinations. Nearly half a century later, when writing his *Personal Memoirs*, Grant recalled his feelings at the time: "A military life had no charms for me, and I had not the faintest idea of staying in the army even if I should be graduated, which I did not expect." He found most of the work uninteresting, though he had an easy aptitude for mathematics and was an outstanding horseman. In the end he did graduate, applied for the cavalry but was rejected because there were no vacancies, and settled for the infantry. Garrison life was boring and he was planning to resign from the army and get a job as a mathematics teacher when the Mexican War broke out in 1846. He strongly disapproved of the war, making no secret of his opinion and later describing it as "one of the most unjust wars ever waged by a stronger against a weaker nation." But at least it was not boring. He played an active role throughout the campaign and got to know most of the men who were to be fellow-commanders of his on the Federal side, or commanders of opposing rebel armies, when the Civil War came along nearly twenty years later.

Soon after his return from Mexico, Grant married a girl he had met at St. Louis, Missouri. A few years later – once more fed up with routine garrison duties and long separations from his wife and two young children – he quit the army to make a modest living as a farmer near St. Louis, later as a clerk in his father's store at Galena, Illinois.

He was a plain, straightforward patriot, with no political skills or sophistication and no great interest in politics until the 1850s when zealots and demagogues on both sides began to tear the country apart over the slavery issue. He was glad, in 1860, that Abraham Lincoln had been voted as the next President because he agreed with Lincoln that the prime issue was not slavery but the maintenance of the United States as a single and united nation. So he had no agonizing choice to make about which side to support in the winter of 1860–1, as one after another the Southern slave states broke away from the Union and declared themselves an independent confederation. Grant was one of those on the Northern side, the vast majority, who thought the whole thing would be over in 90 days.

Grant's Fighting Command

He did not join the first rush of volunteers but made himself useful to the Union cause by helping to organize and drill the new Illinois regiments and ensure that the arsenal at St. Louis did not fall into rebel hands. In the end he could not avoid a return to military life. He was made colonel of the 21st Illinois Regiment. Soon after that, to his surprise, he was promoted to the rank of brigadier general.

Grant was 39 years old, a trained professional soldier with campaigning experience but little relish for army life. No one, in the summer of 1861, could have guessed that he was to become one of the great commanders of the war, comparable to – and ultimately the conqueror of – Robert E. Lee himself. In 1861 he saw action in the western theater in the vicinity of the Mississippi in the state of Missouri, without particularly distinguishing himself.

Early in 1862 he made himself something of a hero in the north by taking Fort Henry on the Tennessee River in a combined army and navy operation, and immediately followed this up by marching on Fort Donelson on the Cumberland River. This was a much tougher proposition and it was not taken without serious setbacks and much ferocious fighting. Here Grant displayed many of the qualities that were to make him such a formidable opponent: the ability to think calmly and clearly in desperate situations, coolness under fire, powers of endurance and tenacity. When the rebel commander finally asked for armistice terms, Grant sent him a prompt and lapidary reply: "No terms except unconditional and immediate surrender can be accepted. I propose to move immediately upon your works." The terms were accepted and Grant seized the fort and took two rebel generals, and 14,000 men prisoner.

It was the first victory of any great substance that the North had had to celebrate. The commanders in Washington, leader-writers for the newspapers, and the public contrasted Grant's aggressive vigor with the cautious and tentative approach being shown by the commander of the Army of the Potomac in the eastern theater. They particularly liked the wording of his surrender letter, and the coincidence of the general's initials with the phrase "unconditional surrender."

Grant was promoted again, to major general, and a few weeks later, in April 1862, he and his army were in action again – this time at Shiloh, another long, pounding, bloody battle in which his determination and sheer doggedness proved the vital factor. In his *Memoirs* he remarked that until Shiloh he had

supposed that one decisive victory would smash the Confederacy. After it, ". . . I gave up the idea of saving the Union except by complete conquest." And he believed the conquest would come, not by taking rebel territory but by destroying rebel armies, as he had done at Fort Donelson.

Grant's Character

To outward appearances Grant was an unlikely commander. He was small in stature and made no effort to look smart. His manner was unassertive. His Illinois soldiers called him "the quiet man" and other people used words such as "plain" and "ordinary." Often enough, he wore nothing to indicate his rank. A fellow-officer described him as being, ". . . entirely free from any pride or hauteur of command." But all the accounts make it clear that when Grant was present there was never any room for doubt about who was in charge. He was a wiry man, tough and neat in movement, always in easy balance. He could be terrible in anger but that was very rare. His voice was pleasant and clear and rarely raised; he never used profane language or betrayed excitement. His orders, spoken or written, were models of force and clarity. A staff officer said, "No matter how hurriedly he might write them on the field, no one ever had the slightest doubt as to their meaning, or ever had to read them over a second time to understand them."

Grant was a practical man, brisk and businesslike. He was not at all pious and hardly ever talked in terms of religious faith or high principles of any kind. He was no great reader and certainly no intellectual, but he had a sharp, natural intelligence, something of Bernard Montgomery's ability to cut through all the confusing complexities and details to the vital, simple core of a problem.

His character rested on a bedrock of honesty, decency and common sense. He had confidence and great vitality and, most importantly, the ability to imbue those around him with the same qualities. He made no apparent effort to impress or ingratiate himself but over the months and years, as he built his army and led it into battle, a very effective relationship grew up between Grant and his staff, corps commanders, officers and men. He cared about his soldiers and looked after them. He cared for the ani-

► *Grant with his wife Julia and their children. This family group photograph was taken in 1868, shortly before Grant was elected President. The eldest boy, Frederick, was 12 at the time of the Vicksburg campaign but managed to see plenty of action.*

mals, too; cruelty to mules or horses was one of the few things that could make him lose his temper. Once a battle was over, he treated captured rebels with compassion and courtesy. The respect he won from his troops enabled him to make heavy demands upon them in the certainty that they would respond.

Not everyone liked him. West Point men of the old style thought he was too informal and scruffy for an army commander. The more intellectual ones equated his simplicity with simple-mindedness. Careerist politician generals – and there were many of them – envied his successes and distrusted his apparent lack of ambition. There were, as always, plenty of journalists on the lookout for flaws in the

hero's character. The best weapon they found to use against him was his undoubted fondness for whiskey.

Grant had first taken seriously to drink in the dreary, garrison-duty years after the Mexican War. He had always been a convivial, unpuritanical man, fond of talking with friends into the night, smoking cigars and enjoying a drink. Now he found escape from the tedium of inactive army service in the whiskey bottle, and sometimes a late-night party would evolve into a bender that went on for days. He maintained the habit in the drifting, unfulfilling years after he left the army. When the Civil War started and he found himself rapidly promoted to the high responsibility of commanding an army,

▲ *John A. Rawlins was an old and trusted friend of Grant's, called in to be his Assistant Adjutant-General, partly to run the administrative side, which* *he did admirably, partly to keep a sharp, restraining eye on the general's famous weakness for hard liquor. He did that admirably too.*

aware of his weakness, he persuaded an old friend, John A. Rawlins, to join him as head of his staff and protector of his better self.

Rawlins was a lawyer and well qualified for both roles. An able and conscientious desk-worker, he was a devoted and fearless enemy of the demon drink. He was also one of the first to see Grant as a potential man of destiny. So he enlisted as a captain and became Grant's Assistant Adjutant General, taking the detailed administrative work off his boss's shoulders, but looming constantly over those shoulders to make sure he kept off the hard liquor. They were together throughout the war and on the whole, despite occasional lapses, the arrangement worked. But this did not halt the flow of rumors and innuendo about the general's weakness for whiskey.

In the bleak winter of 1862–3, when nothing seemed to be going right for the Northern cause, a Pennsylvania politician, A. K. McClure, urged President Lincoln to dismiss Grant. He repeated all the

old accusations. Lincoln, who by this time had heard a lot about Grant but never met him, listened in silence, thought for some time, and then said: "I can't spare this man: he fights."

The Rebel Generals

The unfortunate officer given the job of defending Vicksburg against Grant was Lieutenant General John C. Pemberton. He was an able and conscientious man, good at discipline and administration, but cold in manner, cautious rather than imaginative in his generalship, not in any way inspirational. He was not lucky either. His greatest misfortune, perhaps, was coming up against Grant at the height of his powers. But Pemberton never had the forces to cope with the problem; there were divisions and confusions in the rebel command which worsened as the campaign moved towards its crisis; furthermore, he was a Northerner by origin and the people of the South remembered that, with suspicion.

In her *Diary from Dixie* Mary Boykin Chesnut, whose husband was a military aide to Jefferson Davis, wrote: "Men born Yankees are an unlucky selection as commanders for the Confederacy. They believe in the North in a way no true Southerner ever will, and they see no shame in surrendering to Yankees. They are half-hearted clear through." This was written three months before Pemberton surrendered to Grant at Vicksburg, but Pemberton's is one of the names she cites.

John Pemberton grew up in a Quaker family in Pennsylvania, but from the start he seems to have had a great hankering for the South. He went to West Point, class of 1837, and the friends he made there were nearly all Southerners. He became an outspoken protagonist of states' rights, the belief that the Union was not inviolable and that any state that wanted to had the right to secede. He saw active service in the Mexican War and against the Indians. In 1848 he married a Southern girl from Virginia.

When the Civil War began he was a captain of engineers in the Union army. The War Department in Washington offered him a colonelcy, but although his two brothers were in the Federal army he opted for the Southern cause. Jefferson Davis was impressed by him and gave him a commission in the Confederate army. In the summer of 1862 he

▲ *The Confederate com-*
mander in the field, John
C. Pemberton, was an
experienced and capable

soldier who found himself
out of his depth when he
came up against Grant at
the top of his form.

▲ *"The Gamecock,"*
Joseph E. Johnston, was
given overall command of
the Confederate forces in

Mississippi, but did
nothing to enhance his
military reputation.

commanded at Charleston and in the autumn Davis decided that Pemberton was the man to meet the Northern threat to the Mississippi.

In April 1863, by which time it had become clear that Grant's objective was Vicksburg though which route he would take was still uncertain, another Southern general, senior to Pemberton, was given overall command. This was Joseph E. Johnston, who played a very active and often controversial role throughout the Civil War. Jefferson Davis gave him command of the Confederate forces in Mississippi and Tennessee in the hope that his long experience in war and his undoubted strategic skill would enable him to counter any moves from the North. Grant had a high respect for Johnston's abilities and it was well founded, but Johnston seems to have been oddly out of sorts during the Vicksburg campaign – wrangling with President Davis, unable to join forces with Pemberton, moving too cautiously and making vital decisions too late.

Unlike Grant, Jo Johnston looked every inch an army officer, smart and erect in bearing, with a jaun-

ty manner. His men, who liked him greatly, nicknamed him "the gamecock." He came from a distinguished Virginian family, did well at West Point, fought as an artilleryman against the Indians, then as an engineer officer in the Mexican War. He was a brigadier general when the Civil War broke out. He had not wanted Virginia to secede from the Union but when it did, felt he must offer his services to the Confederacy. It was his timely arrival on the field of First Bull Run in July 1861 that gave victory to the South in the first major battle of the war. But the euphoria of this success was quickly followed by a bad-tempered dispute with Davis, chiefly about the failure of his army to pursue the retreating Northern forces. Johnston always made himself popular with the men under his command, but was a very awkward subordinate, prickly and contentious and inclined to misunderstand his orders. He also had a habit of getting wounded. When he was sent to take charge of the Mississippi front, he was still recovering from severe wounds received at the Battle of Seven Pines in May 1862.

▼ *Confederate soldiers. Left to right: an infantry drummer boy; a private soldier in the infantry; and an ordnance sergeant of the 28th North Carolina Infantry Regiment, holding the regimental Color. (Ron Volstad)*

THE OPPOSING ARMIES

There were men from virtually all the Northern states in Grant's army, but the great majority of them were midwesterners, from Ohio, Iowa and Illinois, Michigan, Wisconsin and Indiana. They were farmers and farmworkers and frontiersmen, fit and tough and practical. Grant grew to be very proud of their steadiness under fire, their ability to endure and stay cheerful, their ingenuity and skills as makeshift engineers. The enemy commander, Jo Johnston, who had fought in the eastern as well as the western sector, also had great respect for them. He warned the Secretary of War in Richmond not to underestimate Grant's soldiers – ". . . his troops are worth double the number of northeastern troops."

Grant's men had signed on for three years. Many of them had seen bitter fighting under his command before the Vicksburg campaign began, but there were many thousands – including all the men newly recruited by General McClernand – who had had no experience of action until they boarded the boats to sail down the Mississippi for the move against Vicksburg.

▼ *Union command of the Mississippi above and below Vicksburg was crucial to the outcome of the campaign. Below:* *Admiral Porter's flagship,* **Black Hawk,** *armed with 9 guns and 2 howitzers.*

Fred B. Schell 85

The Confederate army under General Pemberton was drawn from across the rebel states: Mississippi, Georgia, Alabama, Tennessee, Louisiana and Texas, and most of them – like Grant's troops – were used to hard work in the open air. They were not so ably led as their opponents and, as the campaign gathered pace, their continued defeats and retreats undermined their morale. But they were –

ORDER OF BATTLE: THE ARMY OF THE TENNESSEE

Commander: Major General Ulysses S. Grant
Assistant Adjutant General: John S. Rawlins

XIII ARMY CORPS

Major General John A. McClernand
Major General Edward O. C. Ord
(from 18 June 1863)

9th Division: Brigadier General Peter J. Osterhaus
FIRST BRIGADE: 118th Illinois, 49th Indiana, 69th Indiana, 7th Kentucky, 120th Ohio
SECOND BRIGADE: 54th Indiana, 22nd Kentucky, 16th Ohio, 42nd Ohio, 114th Ohio
CAVALRY: 2nd Illinois, 3rd Illinois, 6th Missouri

10th Division: Brigadier General Andrew J. Smith
FIRST BRIGADE: 16th Indiana, 60th Indiana, 67th Indiana, 83rd Ohio, 96th Ohio, 23rd Wisconsin
SECOND BRIGADE: 77th Illinois, 97th Illinois, 130th Illinois, 19th Kentucky, 48th Ohio

12th Division: Brigadier General Alvin P. Hovey
FIRST BRIGADE: 11th Indiana, 24th Indiana, 34th Indiana, 46th Indiana, 29th Wisconsin
SECOND BRIGADE: 87th Illinois, 47th Indiana, 24th Iowa, 28th Iowa, 56th Ohio

14th Division: Brigadier General Eugene A. Carr
FIRST BRIGADE: 33rd Illinois, 99th Illinois, 8th Indiana, 18th Indiana, 1st U.S. (siege guns)
SECOND BRIGADE: 21st Iowa, 22nd Iowa, 23rd Iowa, 11th Wisconsin

XV ARMY CORPS

Major General William T. Sherman

1st Division: Major General Frederick Steele
FIRST BRIGADE: 13th Illinois, 27th Missouri, 29th Missouri, 30th Missouri, 31st Missouri, 32nd Missouri
SECOND BRIGADE: 25th Iowa, 31st Iowa, 3rd Missouri, 12th Missouri, 17th Missouri, 76th Ohio
THIRD BRIGADE: 4th Iowa, 9th Iowa, 26th Iowa, 30th Iowa

2nd Division: Major General Frank P. Blair
FIRST BRIGADE: 113th Illinois, 116th Illinois, 6th Missouri, 8th Missouri, 13th U.S.
SECOND BRIGADE: 55th Illinois, 127th Illinois, 83rd Indiana, 54th Ohio, 57th Ohio
THIRD BRIGADE: 30th Ohio, 37th Ohio, 47th Ohio, 4th West Virginia

3rd Division: Brigadier General James M. Tuttle
FIRST BRIGADE: 114th Illinois, 93rd Indiana, 72nd Ohio, 95th Ohio
SECOND BRIGADE: 47th Illinois, 5th Minnesota, 11th Missouri, 8th Wisconsin
THIRD BRIGADE: 8th Iowa, 12th Iowa, 35th Iowa

XVII ARMY CORPS

Major General James B. McPherson

3rd Division: Major General John A. Logan
FIRST BRIGADE: 20th Illinois, 31st Illinois, 45th Illinois, 124th Illinois, 23rd Indiana
SECOND BRIGADE: 30th Illinois, 20th Ohio, 68th Ohio, 78th Ohio
THIRD BRIGADE: 8th Illinois, 17th Illinois, 81st Illinois, 7th Missouri, 32nd Ohio

6th Division: Brigadier General John McArthur
FIRST BRIGADE: 1st Kansas, 16th Wisconsin
SECOND BRIGADE: 11th Illinois, 72nd Illinois, 95th Illinois, 14th Wisconsin, 17th Wisconsin
THIRD BRIGADE: 11th Iowa, 13th Iowa, 15th Iowa, 16th Iowa

7th Division: Brigadier General Marcellus M. Crocker
FIRST BRIGADE: 48th Indiana, 59th Indiana, 4th Minnesota, 18th Wisconsin
SECOND BRIGADE: 56th Illinois, 17th Iowa, 10th Missouri, 24th Missouri, 80th Ohio
THIRD BRIGADE: 93rd Illinois, 5th Iowa, 10th Iowa, 26th Missouri

Herron's Division: Major General Francis J. Herron
FIRST BRIGADE: 37th Illinois, 26th Indiana, 20th Iowa, 34th Iowa, 38th Iowa
SECOND BRIGADE: 94th Illinois, 19th Iowa, 20th Wisconsin

Unattached Cavalry: Colonel Cyrus Bussey
5th Illinois, 3rd Iowa, 2nd Wisconsin

These were the three corps that formed Grant's Army of the Tennessee throughout the Vicksburg campaign. The list does not include the reinforcement units that joined the army when Vicksburg was besieged. Grant's total effective force ranged from 43,000 men at the beginning to 75,000 at the close of the campaign. The garrison force left behind at Milliken's Bend, half white, half Negro, was called the African Brigade and was commanded by Colonel Isaac J. Shepard. it comprised six infantry regiments surprisingly – better armed than the Federal troops.

In his *Memoirs* Grant mentions that when Vicksburg finally surrendered he seized, among other things, some 60,000 muskets, and goes on: "The smallarms of the enemy were far superior to the bulk of ours. Up to this time our troops in the West had been limited to the old United States flintlock muskets changed into percussion, or the Belgian musket imported early in the war – almost as dangerous to the person firing it as to the one aimed at – and a few new and improved arms. These were of many different calibers, a fact that caused much trouble in distributing ammunition during an engagement. The enemy had generally new arms which had run the blockade and were of uniform caliber. After the surrender I authorized all colonels whose regiments were armed with inferior muskets, to place them in the stack of captured arms and replace them with the latter."

This is surprising because it is generally assumed that the North, with its vastly stronger industrial capacity, was better able to provide for its soldiers.

By this halfway stage of the Civil War the usual infantry weapon, on both sides, was the Springfield 1855 rifle-musket, which weighed nearly ten pounds, was muzzle-loaded, and which fired a .58 caliber lead bullet through a 40-inch barrel that had been rifled for greater accuracy. The common artillery weapon, again on both sides, was the M 1857 12-pounder gun which could project a round-shot ball up to 2,000 yards. Muzzle-loaded, it could also fire shells or canister. Several other guns were used – howitzers for high-trajectory fire; 6-pounder smoothbores; and various kinds of rifled guns that were more accurate. But artillerymen on both sides felt more at home, and safer, with the smoothbore 12-pounder which was known as the "Napoleon."

ORDER OF BATTLE: THE CONFEDERATE ARMY

VICKSBURG FORCES

Commander: Lieutenant General John C. Pemberton

1st Division: Major General W. W. Loring (most of this division was lost to Pemberton after the battle of Champion Hill and joined forces with General Joseph B. Johnston, who became Pemberton's senior officer in November 1862 but who played only a minor part in the campaign).
FIRST BRIGADE: 6th Mississippi, 15th Mississippi, 20th Mississippi, 23rd Mississippi, 26th Mississippi
SECOND BRIGADE: 3rd Mississippi, 22nd Mississippi, 31st Mississippi, 33rd Mississippi, 1st Mississippi
THIRD BRIGADE: 27th Alabama, 35th Alabama, 54th Alabama, 55th Alabama, 9th Arkansas, 3rd Kentucky, 7th Kentucky, 12th Louisiana

Stevenson's Division: Major General Carter L. Stevenson
FIRST BRIGADE: 40th Georgia, 41st Georgia, 42nd Georgia, 43rd Georgia, 52nd Georgia
SECOND BRIGADE: 20th Alabama, 23rd Alabama, 30th Alabama, 31st Alabama, 46th Alabama
THIRD BRIGADE: 34th Georgia, 36th Georgia, 39th Georgia, 56th Georgia,

57th Georgia
FOURTH BRIGADE: 3rd Tennessee, 31st Tennessee, 43rd Tennessee, 59th Tennessee
TEXAS LEGION

Forney's Division: Major General John H. Forney
HÉBERT'S BRIGADE: 3rd Louisiana, 21st Louisiana, 36th Mississippi, 37th Mississippi, 38th Mississippi, 43rd Mississippi, 7th Mississippi, 2nd Alabama
MOORE'S BRIGADE: 37th Alabama, 40th Alabama, 42nd Alabama, 1st Mississippi, 35th Mississippi, 40th Mississippi, 2nd Texas

Smith's Division: Major General Martin L. Smith
FIRST BRIGADE: 17th Louisiana, 31st Louisiana, 4th Mississippi, 46th Mississippi
VAUGHN'S BRIGADE: 60th Tennessee, 61st Tennessee, 62nd Tennessee
THIRD BRIGADE: 26th Louisiana, 27th Louisiana, 28th Louisiana
MISSISSIPPI STATE TROOPS

Bowen's Division: Major General John S. Bowen
FIRST (MISSOURI) BRIGADE: 1st and 4th Missouri, 2nd Missouri, 3rd Missouri,

5th Missouri, 6th Missouri
SECOND BRIGADE: 15th Arkansas, 19th Arkansas, 20th Arkansas, 21st Arkansas, 1st Arkansas, 12th Arkansas, 3rd Missouri Cavalry

JOHNSTON'S FORCES

Commander: General Joseph E. Johnston

GREGG'S BRIGADE: 3rd Tennessee, 10th and 30th Tennessee, 41st Tennessee, 50th Tennessee, 7th Texas
GIST'S BRIGADE: 46th Georgia, 14th Mississippi, 24th South Carolina
WALKER'S BRIGADE

At its greatest number, including the units that confronted Grant at Raymond and Jackson, Pemberton's army probably numbered just over 40,000 men. In his official report, Pemberton said that his effective total, during the siege of Vicksburg, was not more than 28,000.

According to Johnston's reports, his effective strength at the beginning of June 1863 was 24,000 men.

For the ultimate siege of the city, of course, Grant brought up guns of greater caliber, up to 32 pounds, and also used a navy battery. In the matter of cavalry, Grant had enough for his needs and Pemberton had not, and this was an important factor.

An even more important factor was command of the river and this was Grant's entirely. He had willing and expert support throughout the campaign from Admiral Porter and his sailors and ships, of whom he wrote: "The most perfect harmony reigned between the two arms of the service. There never was a request made, that I am aware of, either of the flag-officer or any of his subordinates, that was not promptly complied with."

◀ *Union soldiers. Left, an infantry private; right, a company quartermaster sergeant of cavalry. (Ron Volstad)*

THE STRATEGIC SITUATION, AUTUMN 1862

The late summer of 1862 saw the high tide of Confederate fortunes. A few months earlier their capital city, Richmond, had seemed to be in grave danger and their armies were falling back in the western sector, too. By September the situation had changed dramatically and it was the northern capital, Washington, that seemed threatened.

In a masterly campaign through northern Virginia, Robert E. Lee had outmaneuvered and bewildered John Pope, the new commander of the Federal Army of Virginia, and then heavily defeated him at the Second Battle of Bull Run. This was only a few miles from Washington. Lee marched north, crossed the Potomac at Harpers Ferry and advanced deep into Maryland. For a few weeks it looked as though Lee's boldness and sheer military skill were going to prevail over the huge advantages that the North enjoyed in terms of manpower and industrial might.

The Union forces were also on the retreat in the west. In the first months of the year Grant's advance along the Tennessee from Fort Donelson to Shiloh had taken him to the borders of the state of Mississippi. There, however, he had been halted and his army was soon heavily depleted by the need to send detachments to east Tennessee where the Southern generals, Braxton Bragg and Kirby Smith, were pushing vigorously northward toward the Ohio River.

It was a desperate time for President Lincoln. There were many in his own Republican Party who thought that he was weak and too much under the influence of his Secretary of State, William H. Seward. There were many people in the North who had never thought the secessionist slave states should be held in the Union by force, and many more who had supported the idea at first, when everyone thought the issue would quickly be settled, but who were now sickened by the bloodshed and waste of the war and who wanted peace even though

it would mean the breakup of the United States.

On 17 September 1862 a battle was fought at Antietam in Maryland that was bloodier than anything that had gone before. In one day the Federal army lost more than 12,000 men. The result was inconclusive, virtually a draw, but the battle did persuade Lee to pull his army back to Virginia. The immediate threat to Washington and Northern territory generally was over, for the moment at least. But Lincoln had another great anxiety. It looked increasingly likely that Britain, in great need of cotton from the Southern states, was about to recognize the Confederacy as an independent state. The Royal Navy would certainly be able to break the blockade of Southern ports and restore the cotton traffic across the Atlantic. As things stood, recognition from London would almost certainly put an end to all hopes of restoring the Union. Lincoln needed victories and he needed them soon.

Grant's First Attempt, November to December 1862

Grant's first scheme for taking Vicksburg was the obvious one. He would march southward, roughly following the line of the Mississippi Central Railroad, by way of Holly Springs, Grenada and Oxford. Another hundred miles or so would bring him to Jackson, Mississippi, and from there, swinging westward, Vicksburg and the river were within easy reach. By this route there were no great natural obstacles to surmount. Grant had some 30,000 men for the advance and reckoned that the Confederate commander, Pemberton, had a similar force. But Grant and his army had victories behind them and felt confident that there were more to come.

His chief anxiety was about his line of supplies. He was venturing deep into enemy territory and the food and ammunition needed to keep his army operative had to reach him by a single-track railroad that

▲ *John A. McClernand was one of those who sought military glory in order to advance his political ambitions. Grant never really trusted* *him, but waited patiently for him to go too far, and then sacked him.*

▲ *Henry W. Halleck was President Lincoln's chief military adviser in Washington throughout the campaign. His lawyer's skill was* *instrumental in keeping McClernand under control.*

could not be continually guarded over its entire length. Another mounting anxiety that had nothing to do with the enemy or the nature of the terrain was the question of what his own divisional commander, General John A. McClernand, was up to. McClernand had been with Grant at Fort Henry and Fort Donelson and Shiloh. He had not greatly impressed Grant but he was a man of powerful political influence and ambition, and in April 1862 he had been promoted to major general (through his political connections) which meant that he outranked every one in the army except Grant himself.

In the late summer McClernand took leave of absence from the army, went to Washington and spoke to President Lincoln. He argued that morale was low in the midwestern states and recruitment was slow, and that he was the man to tour the region,

restore confidence and stimulate recruitment. In return he wanted the President's promise of an independent command, with authority to capture Vicksburg and open up the Mississippi valley. Lincoln agreed, thinking more of the political benefits than of the military disadvantages that might accrue. In October McClernand toured Indiana, Illinois and Iowa, making speeches, gathering recruits, and dispatching the newly formed regiments to Memphis on the Mississippi.

Lincoln's chief military adviser, General Henry W. Halleck, had small respect for McClernand as a soldier and disapproved of the idea of splitting the command in a vital and difficult operation. Halleck, a lawyer by training, saw to it that the written orders to McClernand included the instruction that McClernand should only move to Memphis "when a sufficient force, not required by the operations of General Grant" had been assembled there.

Grant was suspicious of McClernand. In *Personal Memoirs* he recalled his feelings in early November when he was marching his army to Holly Springs: "At this stage of the campaign against Vicksburg I was very much disturbed by newspaper rumors that General McClernand was to have a separate and independent command within mine, to operate against Vicksburg by way of the Mississippi River. Two commanders on the same field are always one too many, and in this case I did not think the general selected had either the experience or the qualifications to fit him for so important a position."

On 10 November Grant sent a message to Halleck in Washington, asking for clarification. The reply was reassuring: "You have command of all the troops sent to your department and have permission to fight the enemy where you please." So Grant set up a supply base at Holly Springs, left a garrison of 1,500 men there to protect it, and marched south, meeting no real resistance. At Oxford he paused and revised his plan.

His most trusted commander, and by this time a close friend, was Major General William Tecumseh Sherman, an Ohio man and a fighting commander of great experience. On 8 December Grant ordered Sherman to bring his division back to Memphis as quickly as possible, take charge of the recruits McClernand had sent there, then sail down the Mississippi to threaten Vicksburg from the north in cooperation with the navy's gunboats. The scheme had two advantages. It would preempt any move that McClernand was planning to make against Vicksburg. And it would fix Pemberton on the horns of a dilemma. Should he fall back with the bulk of his army to meet the threat from Sherman? Or rely on Vicksburg's natural defenses and small garrison, and keep his main force 70 miles to the northeast, confronting Grant? In the event, the decision was taken for Pemberton.

Sherman moved off for Memphis with his usual brisk efficiency. Grant resumed his southward march with two divisions. On 20 December disaster struck. The rebel commander, Earl Van Dorn, leading 3,500 cavalrymen, attacked Grant's supply depot at Holly Springs, seized it and destroyed great quantities of food, forage and ammunition. Another

▲ *Nathan Bedford Forrest, one of the dashing Confederate cavalry leaders whose raids behind the Federal front lines forced Grant to* *abandon his first attempt to march on Vicksburg.*

Confederate cavalry leader, the legendary Nathan Bedford Forrest, had already been ranging and raiding across northern Mississippi and western Tennessee, destroying rail and telegraph communications, taking arms and horses, enrolling fresh recruits, and generally creating havoc in Grant's rear. The destruction of his supplies at Holly Springs was the final straw. Grant pulled out of Oxford, heading north again, on 21 December.

At that time it was a generally accepted axiom that an army operating in enemy territory must secure its supplies and communications. Grant sent detachments out in all directions, with all the wagons they could lay hands on, to bring back food and forage from farms in the vicinity. "I was amazed," he was to recall, "at the quantity of supplies the country afforded. It showed that we could have

▼ *Uniforms of the Federal army. Left to right: a captain of light artillery; an artillery corporal; and a regimental quartermaster sergeant of the heavy artillery. (Ron Volstad)*

subsisted off the country for two months instead of two weeks . . . This taught me a lesson which was taken advantage of later in the campaign." The lesson he had learned, he thought, more than compensated for the disappointment of failing in his first attempt to get at Vicksburg.

Sherman's Attack at Chickasaw Bluffs

The destruction of his telegraph lines meant that Grant's orders did not get through for several days. So Sherman went on believing that Grant was near Grenada, holding the attention of Pemberton and the greater part of his army. Consequently, as soon as Sherman reached Memphis he set about organizing McClernand's new regiments into brigades and divisions, and arranging the transportation of his army – grown to more than 30,000 men – down the Mississippi.

The Union's naval commander in the area was Admiral David Porter, a stocky little man of drive and vigor. He got on well with Sherman and the

▼ *Rear Admiral David D. Porter, commander of Grant's naval forces* *throughout the campaign and a pillar of strength and support.*

expedition was quickly planned. By 26 December Sherman's army, in four divisions, was landing on the southern bank of the Yazoo, seven miles north of the city of Vicksburg. General Pemberton arrived on the scene at much the same time. Having realized that Grant was withdrawing, and having received reports that the Union navy was reconnoitering the Yazoo near the point where it joins the Mississippi, Pemberton had acted with dispatch. He moved brigades from Grenada and men and guns from the Vicksburg garrison, and set them up along the summit slopes of the long line of cliffs, the Chickasaw Bluffs, that commanded the ground Sherman's men would have to cross.

It was an ideal defensive position and Pemberton must have been surprised and grateful that Sherman had chosen this route. The attackers would have to push their way through a tangled maze of lakes, swamps and bayous (marshy offshoots of the river), in full view of the defenders, before hurling themselves at the steep slopes of the Bluffs. There had been much recent rainfall and the waters were high, and more than half of Sherman's men had never been in action before. It is difficult to understand why Sherman attacked – until one remembers that he was still under the impression

PLAN OF FORT HINDMAN

THE APPEARANCE OF THE CASEMATES BEFORE THE ATTACK.

CASEMATE N° 2 DESTROYED BY U.S. GUNBOAT LOUISVILLE.

that Pemberton's main force was 70 miles away to the northeast, and that he was anxious to get the job done before McClernand arrived to grab the glory.

The attack was launched on the morning of 29 December; the attackers were midwesterners, from Iowa, Illinois and Ohio. They had to force their way, as one of the divisional commanders described it, ". . . through the mucky and tangled swamp, under a withering fire of grape, canister, shells and Miniéballs." The defenders – slightly outnumbered but securely dug into commanding positions – were regiments from Georgia, Alabama, Tennessee, Mississippi and Louisiana. The result was inevitable. Sherman's men were beaten back with the loss of

208 killed, 1,005 wounded and 563 missing. The Confederate losses were less than one-eighth of that number: 63 killed, 134 wounded and 10 missing. Sherman later complained that some of his units had shown cowardice. One of his divisional commanders, Brigadier General George W. Morgan, hotly repudiated the charge and accused Sherman of rashly attacking at the point where the enemy's defenses were strongest.

Sherman pulled his army back to the Yazoo, got his men on to the boats and withdrew to Milliken's Bend on the west bank of the Mississippi, some 20 miles above Vicksburg. There he conferred with Admiral Porter and they decided to sail northward, turn up the Arkansas River and destroy the troublesome Confederate stronghold Fort Hindman. It was at this moment that an angry and impatient General McClernand landed in their midst.

McClernand had had a bad time. His recruiting drive in the midwest states had gone well but he had begun to get worried when the order to go to Memphis and lead his army downriver to the seizure of Vicksburg did not come. In mid-December he sent urgent inquiries to Washington. The replies were not reassuring. He was to have command of the Mississippi operation but not as an independent army commander, as he had expected, but merely as the commander of an army corps under General Grant's supervision. So he needed orders from Grant before he could move. Grant dutifully sent the orders, under instruction from Washington, but this was one of his messages that did not get through because the telegraph wires had been cut. McClernand could only wait and worry. On 23 December he telegraphed again to Washington and at last secured the order to proceed to Memphis.

McClernand Takes Over

He arrived there hurriedly on 28 December, but too late. Sherman had already sailed, with the whole army, for Vicksburg. By now McClernand was convinced that there was a high-level conspiracy to frustrate his ambitions, by Halleck in Washington and Grant in the field. The conviction grew upon him as time passed, but he was never able to prove anything. In his *Personal Memoirs* Grant tells the

◀ *Chickasaw Bayou and the bluffs, after a contemporary sketch; in the foreground, the artillery are guns of General Morgan L. Smith's 2nd Division.*

▼ *Porter's gunboats bombarding Port Hindman into submission – as recorded in the pages of* **Harper's Weekly.**

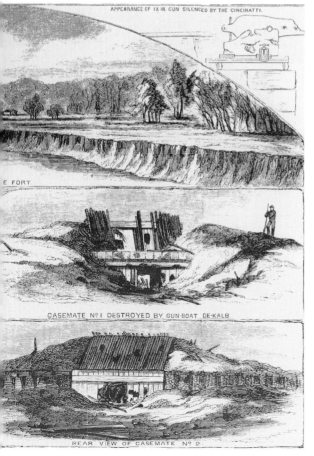

APPEARANCE OF IX IN. GUN SILENCED BY THE CINCINATTI.

E FORT

CASEMATE Nº I DESTROYED BY GUN-BOAT DE-KALB

REAR VIEW OF CASEMATE Nº 2

story laconically and then adds: "I had good reason to believe that in forestalling him I was by no means giving offence to those whose authority to command was above both him and me."

It was into the New Year, 2 January 1863, when McClernand finally caught up with his army at Milliken's Bend. He showed his orders to Sherman and took charge, naming his force "the Army of the Mississippi." He formed it into two corps, giving Sherman command of one of them. Sherman outlined the idea of a raid against Fort Hindman and McClernand liked it. They sailed up the Arkansas and bombarded the fort which quickly surrendered. Five thousand Confederate troops and seventeen guns were taken.

By this time General Grant was in the area and on 17 January he visited McClernand and his army: "It was here made clear to me," he later wrote, "that both the army and navy were so distrustful of McClernand's fitness to command that, while they would do all they could to ensure success, this distrust was an element of weakness."

Grant had no alternative but to take charge himself. If he did not, he would have to leave McClernand in command, and he did not trust him to make a success of it. It was this rogue element, the McClernand factor, that determined the shape of the Vicksburg campaign. The attack would be made down the Mississippi and it would be led by Ulysses S. Grant.

◀ *Nathan P. Banks was the Union commander in Louisiana. His importance in the Vicksburg story was entirely negative. He was conspicuous only for his continued absence from the scene of action.*

GRANT'S WINTER PROBLEMS

For the North, the winter of 1862–3 was one of profound discontent. Lincoln had three great armies in the field – in Virginia, Tennessee and on the Mississippi – but there had been no victories to celebrate, and one resounding defeat, at Fredericksburg, Virginia, on 13 December. The midterm elections of 1862 had gone badly for the President's Republican Party. And those in the North who wanted peace at any price were gaining in numbers and in confidence. Meanwhile, in the Mississippi valley the cold rain came relentlessly down, the rivers rose and turned brown with mud, dry places became creeks and marshes .

On paper, the situation of the Northern forces on the Mississippi looked strong and promising. They controlled the river from its source to the cliffs of Vicksburg and they had control of it, too, as it approached the Gulf of Mexico in the south. Admiral Farragut had stormed past the rebel forts and taken New Orleans in the spring of 1862, and by the end of the year the Federals had an army of some 30,000 men, commanded by Major General Nathan P. Banks, in Louisiana. The obvious strategy was for Banks to push northward up the river, take Port Hudson and then press on to threaten Vicksburg from the south, while Grant closed in from the north. But Banks – at first preoccupied with establishing firm and incorrupt control over New Orleans, then with suppressing active rebel bands in southern Louisiana – set off up the Red River, heading northwestward and away from the Mississippi. Grant realized that he was not going to get any help from Banks.

He now had some 40,000 men camped along the west bank of the river, on the gentle crescent known as Milliken's Bend, a few miles above Vicksburg. Their tents had to be pitched in foul-smelling mud, alive with frogs and crawfish. There was much sickness in the camps, some deaths and some desertions. Grant decided that the best thing for the men's health and morale would be to give them work to do. He would do this in such a way as to keep Pemberton uncertain as to his line of approach. "The problem," Grant said, "was to secure a footing upon dry ground on the east side of the river from which the troops could operate against Vicksburg." To this end he launched three projects, each of which would keep his soldiers and sailors hard at work and involve a great deal of hydraulic engineering.

First and Second Projects

As it approaches Vicksburg, the river swings round in a tight loop, almost doubling back on itself – one moment it is running northeast, but very soon it runs southwest and past the Vicksburg bluffs. A long narrow peninsula lay between the two stretches of river. If a north-south channel were to be dug across the neck of this peninsula and if the river could then be persuaded to swing into this channel and follow a new course, Vicksburg with all its wharves, warehouses and gun emplacements would be left high and dry and entirely pointless, either as a military stronghold or as a commercial center. The idea appealed to the Mississippi veteran, Abraham Lincoln, and Grant was happy to give it a go. He set men of Sherman's 15th Army Corps to work, digging and dredging. They built a dam at the northern end, in the hope that when this was removed the river would pour through with sufficient weight to gouge out a deep new channel for itself. This, however, did not happen. On 8 March the river rose so high that it broke through and over the dam of its own volition, then spread out far and wide, flooding camps and drowning horses. Most of the Mississippi stayed on its old course.

Some 50 miles above Vicksburg, on the western side of the river and very close to it, lay a sizable stretch of water called Lake Providence. Only a levee (embankment) separated the river from the lake. The idea was that if the levee were breached, the level of the lake would rise, helping to make it practicable, at the farther end of the lake, to force a navigable channel through the express swamps and many streams and rivers so that flat-bottomed steamboats and transports might negotiate the 200-mile trip to regain the Mississippi far to the south of Vicksburg.

Grant thought this idea stood a better chance than the first and a division of XVII Army Corps was put to the task. This corps was commanded by Major General James B. McPherson, a young man of high promise and engaging personality. He had joined Grant just over a year before, when they were marching to take Fort Henry. McPherson was a lieutenant colonel of engineers at that time, and he impressed Grant and Sherman throughout the campaigning that followed and gained rapid promotion. He was bright, quick and reliable, and greatly trusted by Grant. He was also full of bounce and fun, and made the most of the Lake Providence opportunity. He had a tugboat hauled to the lake overland, set up his headquarters on board and enjoyed some convivial evenings, cruising along with plenty to drink and the band playing.

His men liked the lake, too – the fishing was excellent – but they did not enjoy it so much when they had to start hacking a channel through the thickly vegetated wetlands beyond. They had to remove trees and sunken tree stumps from deep water and marshes. Gradually, the going slowed to a

◀ *Grant's astonishing attempt to evade the Vicksburg guns by changing the course of the Mississippi River involved weeks of heavy digging by soldiers and gangs of Negro laborers. It was futile. The river simply could not be diverted.*

▶ *Above right: The Mississippi River refusing to cooperate with the first of Grant's winter projects.*

▶ *Below right: Confederate transports taking cattle to Vicksburg.*

crawl and then ground to a halt. It was the end of the second project.

Third Project

Other routes were tried, similar to the Lake Providence scheme but on the eastern side of the Mississippi. The first to be attempted was by way of the Yazoo Pass, an area of swamps and streams about 200 miles north of Vicksburg, which led to a complex river system and finally to the Yazoo River itself. An amphibious expedition following this route could put an army on to dry land a few miles north

of Vicksburg, giving Grant the choice of attacking the Chickasaw Bluffs again or swinging eastward to get at Vicksburg from that side.

In late February his engineers exploded a mine in the embankment and let the swollen waters of the Mississippi flood through the Yazoo Pass. Two ironclad gunboats and many smaller naval craft, followed by transports carrying 4,500 troops, set off on a long, circuitous voyage. They soon ran into trouble. Marauding rebels chopped down trees to block their progress and these had to be hauled out of the way by manpower, one at a time. Overhanging branches knocked the ships' smokestacks down. Underwater

Grant's Attempts to Approach Vicksburg, Dec 1862-March 1863

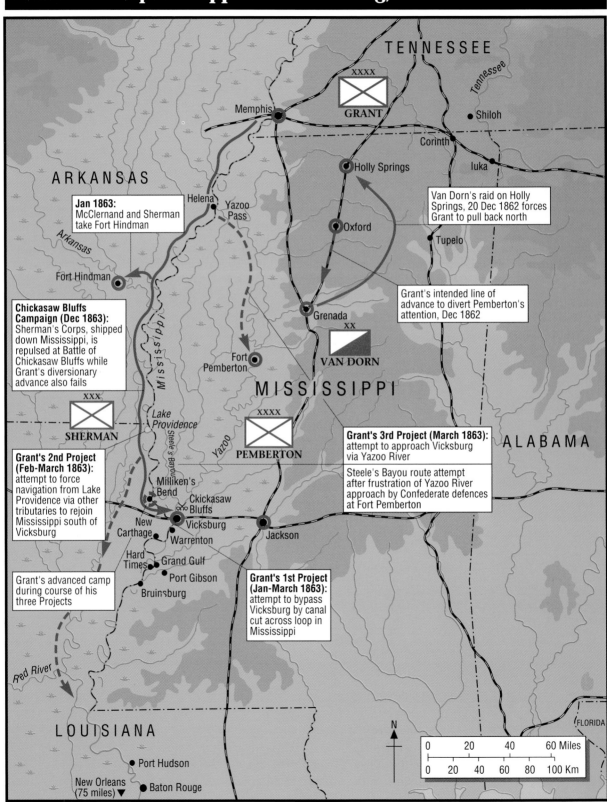

Jan 1863:
McClernand and Sherman take Fort Hindman

Van Dorn's raid on Holly Springs, 20 Dec 1862 forces Grant to pull back north

Grant's intended line of advance to divert Pemberton's attention, Dec 1862

Chickasaw Bluffs Campaign (Dec 1863):
Sherman's Corps, shipped down Mississippi, is repulsed at Battle of Chickasaw Bluffs while Grant's diversionary advance also fails

Grant's 2nd Project (Feb-March 1863):
attempt to force navigation from Lake Providence via other tributaries to rejoin Mississippi south of Vicksburg

Grant's 3rd Project (March 1863):
attempt to approach Vicksburg via Yazoo River

Steele's Bayou route attempt after frustration of Yazoo River approach by Confederate defences at Fort Pemberton

Grant's advanced camp during course of his three Projects

Grant's 1st Project (Jan-March 1863):
attempt to bypass Vicksburg by canal cut across loop in Mississippi

TENNESSEE

ARKANSAS

MISSISSIPPI

ALABAMA

LOUISIANA

FLORIDA

Memphis
Shiloh
Corinth
Iuka
Holly Springs
Helena
Yazoo Pass
Oxford
Tupelo
Fort Hindman
Grenada
Fort Pemberton
Lake Providence
Steele's Bayou
Yazoo
Milliken's Bend
Ckickasaw Bluffs
New Carthage
Vicksburg
Warrenton
Jackson
Hard Times
Grand Gulf
Port Gibson
Bruinsburg
Red River
Port Hudson
New Orleans (75 miles)
Baton Rouge

XXXX GRANT
XX VAN DORN
XXX SHERMAN
XXXX PEMBERTON

0	20	40	60 Miles
0	20 40 60	80	100 Km

tree stumps threatened to hole the vessels. Sometimes the current was so strong that the ships were virtually out of control. At other times, in shallow, sluggish waters, blocked with rotten stumps and driftwood, the flotilla could only inch its way forward. They were plagued by mosquitoes. When they finally gained the Yazoo they found the way ahead denied them by rebel guns, set up on a sector of dry ground which the Confederates called Fort Pemberton. The river was narrow at this point which meant that the ships could not maneuver to

bring their full firepower to bear, and the rebel gunners could deal with them at leisure. They retreated.

Admiral Porter now suggested that a shorter way to the Yazoo, avoiding Fort Pemberton, might be found by way of a backwater called Steele's Bayou. This was another winding, circuitous route but Grant was still full of hope and confidence. He wrote to a friend: ". . . we are going through a campaign here such as has not been heard of on this continent before." Porter pushed ahead, using his

The maze of marshes, creeks and waterways, set in dense woodlands north of Vicksburg, presented Grant's engineers, soldiers and sailors with apparently endless obstacles. Hundreds of makeshift bridges (above) had to be built. Above right: rafts were constructed to get troops across deep creeks. Right: Porter's gunboats and transports often had to hack their way through felled trees and haul out underwater obstructions, usually in semidarkness, sometimes under Confederate fire.

gunboats as battering rams to smash a way through the trees. Sailors had to stand by with brooms to sweep the decks clear of all the small creatures that tumbled down from overhanging branches – racoons, squirrels, fledgling birds. Rebel snipers lurked in the undergrowth. Things got worse and when the sound of trees being felled across the river behind them could be heard, it was realized that the task was hopeless. Suddenly there was a real danger of the entire fleet being surrounded and trapped – in a forest. Some of Sherman's regiments came to the rescue, driving the rebels off and removing the trees, then hauling the boats backward until the channel was wide enough for them to turn around and go back under their own power.

Spring was coming, the rains had stopped and the floodwaters were subsiding. Grant and his men had been laboring hard, often in dreadful conditions, for more than two months and they were no closer to solving the Vicksburg problem than they had been when they began. There were rumblings and grumblings in the army, and savage attacks on Grant in the scurrilous Northern newspapers revived the old charge of drunkenness and called for his replacement.

But the top men in Washington kept their faith in him. In his *Personal Memoirs* he wrote: "With all the pressure brought to bear on them, both President Lincoln and General Halleck stood by me to the end of the campaign. I had never met Mr. Lincoln, but his support was constant." In military terms, it might have made better sense to pull the whole force, still called the Army of the Tennessee, back to Memphis and start again from there. To most people, though, North and South, this would look like defeat. The President had made it clear that he wanted Vicksburg taken by the river line, and Grant was a determined man, no easy quitter. In his office aboard the steamer *Magnolia*, moored by Milliken's Bend, he spent many hours wreathed in cigar smoke, poring over his maps, thinking.

▼ *Porter's fleet at the point where the Yazoo River meets the Mississippi.*

THE MARCH BEGINS

Toward the end of March 1863, as it grew increasingly clear that his water engineering projects were coming to nothing, Grant ordered McClernand to send a reconnaissance party south from Milliken's Bend to see if a road could be found to the banks of the Mississippi somewhere below Vicksburg and well beyond the reach of its guns.

The 69th Indiana Regiment was assigned the task and they set off one fine spring morning, supported by cavalry, a field battery and engineers with bridge-building gear. The floodwaters were receding but there was still plenty of water and mud about. A few small rebel patrols were easily driven off, and the march went reasonably smoothly and took the men to New Carthage on the west bank of the river and well below Vicksburg. It was thought that it would be possible to cross the river at this point and gain the dry higher ground on the east bank, which had been Grant's objective all along. But he would need a fleet of transports and navy gunboats to protect them.

Grant discussed the problem with Admiral Porter who felt confident that he could get the boats past the guns of Vicksburg without crippling losses because the fast current would give them the necessary speed. He warned, however, that it would be a committing move. His ironclad gunboats, known as "turtles," were heavy and underpowered and it would be inviting disaster to try to run them upstream under the rebel gun emplacements.

Grant's generals, especially Sherman, thought that it would be a very risky business. He condemned the plan as "unmilitary" and did not think that it could possibly succeed. If the army did manage to land on the eastern bank of the river, it would be hundreds of miles deep in enemy territory, cut off from lines of supply and communications, an invitation to be surrounded and destroyed. They should all go back to Memphis, Sherman said, and try again by the original route along the line of the Mississippi Central Railroad. Grant had a high regard for Sherman's military sense, but now he was determined to go ahead with the scheme. In his book *This Hallowed Ground*, Bruce Catton writes: "It was perhaps the crucial federal military decision of the war; and it was made by a slouchy little man who never managed to look like a great captain, who had a casual unbuttoned air about him and seemed to be nothing much more than a middle-aged person who used to be a clerk in a small-town harness shop – a man who unexpectedly combined dogged determination with a gambler's daring."

On 29 March Grant ordered McClernand to march his army corps, all four divisions, to the New Carthage area. One division with its artillery was there by 6 April, but the last part of their march had been greatly impeded by flooded roads and fields. So McClernand prospected a new route, farther to the west, that would make the march easier for the rest of the army. It meant constructing several bridges across marshy land, two of them more than 200 yards in length. Grant later wrote proudly: "The river falling made the current in these bayous very rapid, increasing the difficulty of building and permanently fastening these bridges; but the ingenuity of the Yankee soldier was equal to any emergency. The bridges were soon built of such materials as could be found nearby, and so substantial were they that not a single mishap occurred in crossing all the army with artillery, cavalry and wagon trains, except the loss of one siege gun."

The Ships Run Through

In Vicksburg, the Confederate commander, General John Pemberton, was becoming a confused man. His resounding victory over Sherman at the Chickasaw Bluffs at the end of December 1862 had made him so confident that he cheerfully obeyed the call to help General Bragg in central Tennessee and sent

Admiral Porter's fleet successfully ran past the Vicksburg batteries on the night of 16 April 1863, each gunboat with a loaded barge lashed to its starboard side. Confederates on the west bank lit fires to make the ships easier targets for the Vicksburg guns, but even so only one ironclad failed to get through. It was to be a key success. From now on Vicksburg would be open to attack from dry ground to the south and east of the city.

▶ *Porter's flotilla arriving below Vicksburg on the night of 16 April. In the foreground, General Sherman is being rowed to the 16-gun* **Benton**. *Below: two more illustrations depicting the passage of the Vicksburg batteries.*

off three-quarters of his cavalry, men he would miss sorely in the coming struggle. Then came Grant's persistent probings along the waterways to the north and west of Vicksburg in the first months of 1863. Pemberton had no way of knowing which of these moves was seriously intended, which were feints. The only clear thing was that Grant and his army were still active.

By the end of March, though, all the signs were that Grant's efforts in the waterways had come to nothing. Reports reached Pemberton of many empty boats hurrying down the Mississippi to Milliken's Bend. Then he heard from President Davis in Richmond that it looked as though the Federal army in central Tennessee was being reinforced for a major offensive. This would explain the activity on the river – Grant was pulling back to the north. By 12 April Pemberton was so sure this was the explanation that he promised to dispatch a further 8,000 men to help Bragg in Tennessee. Immediately, he began to have second thoughts. There were no reports of loaded boats heading north from Milliken's Bend, and disturbing reports of McClernand's men mending roads and building bridges across the river below New Carthage. On 16 April Pemberton sent off another message to his superiors saying that he was not so sure now that Grant was thinking of retreat. This was the day on which Grant made his clinching move and it had nothing to do with retreat.

Admiral David Porter had made careful preparation for running his fleet past the Vicksburg batteries. He had eight ironclad gunboats and three steamers loaded with stores. Each vessel had a barge full of coal lashed to its starboard side, the side away from the Confederate guns. The great danger was fire spreading from the ships' boilers so these were packed round with bales of cotton, hay and grain, all soaked in water. The decks in front of the boilers were protected in the same way. In the holds men stood ready to cram wads of cotton into shot holes in the hull.

It was important to take the enemy by surprise so the attack would be made at night. The ships would carry no lights. For signaling purposes they had dimmed lanterns, specially hooded so that the light would not be visible to the enemy gunners. It was also important to maintain maximum silence until the enemy spotted them and opened fire, so Porter banished all poultry and pets and ordered his captains to steam at low speed, relying on the river's strong current to provide most of the propulsion. The admiral's flagship, *Benton*, would lead the way, the ships proceeding in line ahead, 50 yards apart, each captain steering slightly to the left of the boat ahead so as to be able to avoid it if it were disabled.

Moorings were slipped at 10:30 on the night of 16 April, a clear, cloudless night with the stars twinkling above. It was very dark at the river level. High above them, as they rounded the sharp bend in the river, they could see the lights of their ultimate objective, the city of Vicksburg, where many of Pemberton's officers and some of the local citizens were attending a dance to celebrate their supposed victory over Grant. The festivities were interrupted by the sudden roar of their guns opening up on the Federal fleet. The Confederates had pickets posted on the far bank of the river and they set fire to derelict buildings to illuminate the water and give their gunners a better view of the targets.

Grant watched the first part of the operation from the deck of his headquarters steamer, and had brought his wife Julia and their two sons to enjoy the show. The elder son, Frederick Dent Grant, was only twelve years old but was allowed to witness much of the Vicksburg campaign from close quarters. More than 30 years later, Fred, as he was known to everyone, reminisced about the experience in a magazine article: "About 10 p.m. all lights were put out, and the fleet started down the river. Suddenly a rocket went up from the shore; a cannon blazed forth from Warrenton; and a shot passed directly in front of our boat. We stopped; a lurid flame sprang up from a house at De Soto, opposite Vicksburg, then another on the river front, and soon fires were burning along the whole front of the city, and the river was lighted as if by sunlight . . . The *Benton* and the other gunboats, steaming up near the city, sent shot and shell pouring into Vicksburg. The transports kept over toward the Louisiana shore, and one – the *Henry Clay* – was set on fire by a redhot shell, and burned to the water's edge . . . The people of Vicksburg lined the hills, and manifested great excitement. On board our boat my father and I stood side by side on the hurricane deck. He was quietly smoking, but an intense light shone in his eyes."

Grant was delighted with the night's work. All the ships had been hit, some of them slightly damaged but nothing that could not be repaired quickly. The *Henry Clay* was the only serious loss.

And the die was now cast. He was committed to going for Vicksburg from the downriver side, even if it meant operating in enemy country without secure lines of supply and communication. Grant was a man of unusual vitality and confidence, but from now until the end of the campaign he displayed these qualities with even greater intensity. One of his officers said of him: "None who had known him the previous years could recognize him as being the same man . . . From this time his genius and his energies seemed to burst forth with new life."

Grant got Sherman to make a convincing feint along the Yazoo to persuade Pemberton that he was about to be attacked from the north. He ordered Colonel Benjamin Grierson, who had been a music teacher before the war and would much rather have been an infantryman than a cavalry commander, to lead three cavalry regiments on a great rampage through the territory east of Vicksburg, destroying communications and stores. Grierson set off from

Memphis on 17 April and ended up, tattered but triumphant, at Baton Rouge in the far south sixteen days later, having ridden 600 miles and created havoc and consternation in his wake.

The day after the successful passage of his ships, Grant went to see how McClernand's routefinding march was progressing. Pleased with what he found, he returned to his headquarters to compose the orders for the all-important march southward. They were dated 20 April. The aim, Grant said, was ". . . to obtain a foothold on the east bank of the Mississippi River, from which Vicksburg can be approached by practicable roads." The order of march would be: McClernand's XIII Army Corps; McPherson's XVII; and Sherman's XV. They would have to travel light, without tents. For the time being men and officers would have to bivouac.

Grant knew that from now on supplies were going to be a serious problem. Ammunition had to

▼ *The Union cavalry leader Benjamin Grierson leads his weary regiments in triumphant procession into Baton Rouge after rampaging through the territory east of Vicksburg, destroying Confederate stores and communications. In sixteen days they covered 600 miles.*

Naval uniforms of the Union. Left to right: a quartermaster; a corporal of the Marine Corps; and a lieutenant commander. (Ron Volstad)

be the first priority. He remembered how the food and forage had poured in when he was retreating from Oxford, four months earlier, and his supply lines had been destroyed and he had sent his men out to get what they could from the surrounding farmlands. They would have to do the same now but they would do it, Grant determined, with control and courtesy. His orders stated: "Commanders are authorized and enjoined to collect all the beef cattle, corn and other necessary supplies on the line of march; but wanton destruction of property, taking of articles useless for military purposes, insulting citizens, going in and searching houses without proper orders from division commanders are positively prohibited. All such irregularities must be summarily punished."

Any immediate worries Grant may have had about provisioning his men and horses over the next week or two were dispersed on the night of 22 April when another convoy swept past the Vicksburg guns. Once again it was a night operation. The convoy consisted of six river steamers, each heavily loaded and towing two equally loaded barges. The steamers were civilian craft and most of their crews had refused to take the risk. So Grant asked for volunteers from his army and was delighted to hear that many more men than were needed had volunteered. "Most of them," he later wrote, "were from Logan's division [of McPherson's army corps], composed generally of men from the southern part of Illinois and from Missouri. All but two of the steamers were commanded by volunteers from the army, and all but one so manned. In this instance, as in all others during the war, I found that volunteers could be found in the ranks and among the commissioned officers to meet every call for aid whether mechanical or professional."

With every day that passed, he was growing more and more proud of the men under his command. Spirits were high. They were happy to be out of the mud and the marshes at last and on their way to Vicksburg, though no one – not even Grant, at this point – knew which route they would take.

Crossing the River

Grant's first plan was to make the crossing in the region of the Confederate fort at Grand Gulf.

Porter's gunboats would knock out the enemy batteries on the cliffs there, then men of McClernand's corps – some 10,000 of them, close-packed on the transports – would land and take the fort.

Eight gunboats moved into the attack at 8 a.m. on 29 April. They fought hard until 1:30 p.m. but failed to silence any of the Confederate guns. Porter lost eighteen sailors killed and 56 wounded, most of them gunners in his flagship which had been hit by a shell between decks. That night Porter got his whole fleet past the guns of Grand Gulf under cover of darkness, while McClernand's men went ashore again on the west bank of the river, then marched through the night to meet the ships a few miles downriver.

Grant had a lucky break that same night. He had only poor and unreliable maps of the land on the east side of the river, so any decision about the best place to make the landing there had to be largely guesswork. Soon after nightfall, though, a small party of Illinois men rowed quietly across the river, cast about the farms, and took prisoner a Negro slave who seemed to be sensible and who knew the region well. They carried him back to Grant, who questioned the man closely. From his replies, it became apparent that the best landing place was Bruinsburg, a few miles further down the river. There were no Confederate defenses there, and by far the best road in the area ran eastward, from Bruinsburg to Port Gibson, where they would be able to cross the flooded Bayou Pierre to threaten Grand Gulf from the rear. To discourage Pemberton from sending reinforcements to Grand Gulf, Grant had asked Sherman to stage another aggressive display along the Yazoo. Done without the loss of a single man, it proved entirely successful.

Before daybreak on 30 April the whole of McClernand's XIII Corps and two brigades of Logan's division of XVII Corps, who had been marching through the night, went aboard the ships once more. At first light they moved quietly downstream to land, unopposed, at Bruinsburg. In his *Personal Memoirs*, Grant recalled the marvelous moment: "When this was effected I felt a degree of relief scarcely ever equaled since. Vicksburg was not yet taken it is true, nor were its defenders demoralized by any of our previous moves. I was now in the enemy's country, with a vast river and the strong-

hold of Vicksburg between me and my base of supplies. But I was on dry ground on the same side of the river with the enemy. All the campaigns, labors, hardships and exposures from the month of December previous to this time that had been made and endured, were for the accomplishment of this one object."

Grant had some 20,000 men ashore and the rest of McPherson's corps coming up close behind.

▲ *Top: an artist's impression of the unsuccessful naval attack on Grand Gulf on the morning of 29 April 1863.*

▲ *Above: toward the end of the bombardment of Grand Gulf. The Union ships, from left to right,* are: **Benton** *(16 guns)*, **Tuscumbia** *(5 guns)*, **Louisville** *(13 guns, 1 howitzer)*, **Carondelet** *(13 guns, 1 howitzer)*, **Pittsburgh** *(12 guns, 1 howitzer)*, **Mound City** *(13 guns, 1 howitzer) and* **Lafayette** *(6 guns, 4 howitzers).*

Crossing the Mississippi

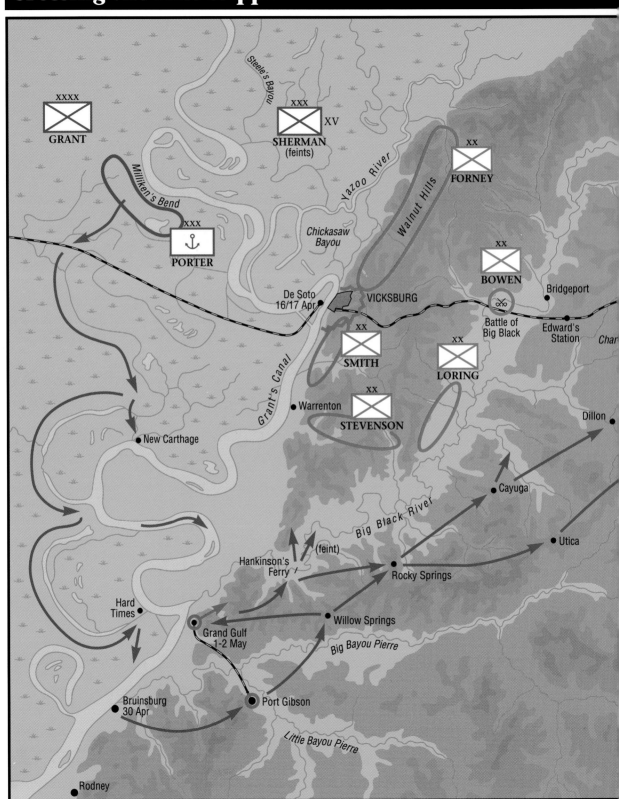

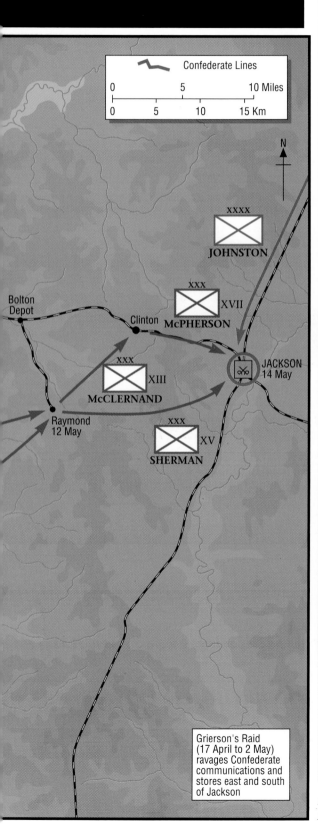

Confederate Lines

| 0 | | 5 | | 10 Miles |
| 0 | 5 | 10 | 15 Km | |

N

xxxx
JOHNSTON

xxx
XVII
McPHERSON

Bolton
Depot

Clinton

xxx
XIII
McCLERNAND

JACKSON
14 May

Raymond
12 May

xxx
XV
SHERMAN

Grierson's Raid
(17 April to 2 May)
ravages Confederate
communications and
stores east and south
of Jackson

▲ *Major General John A. Logan was one of General
McPherson's outstanding brigade commanders.*

Orders had gone to Sherman to leave the Yazoo and hurry after them. But Grant knew that he would be seriously outnumbered if Pemberton gathered all the forces available to him and quick-marched them down to the defense of Grand Gulf. He had to move fast. McClernand's men, who must have been very tired by now, marched eastward toward Port Gibson during the night, and came up against the Confederate outposts before daybreak on 1 May.

There were some 6,000 Confederate troops at Port Gibson under the command of Brigadier General J. S. Bowen. He had sent Pemberton urgent appeals for reinforcements but none had arrived, so he was hopelessly outnumbered. Despite this, Bowen put up a resistance that impressed Grant and induced him to go forward himself and organize the attack. By nightfall Bowen's men were in retreat. Grant urged his weary soldiers a further two miles along the road. Then they were allowed to bivouac for the night. Grant's pride in his men was further strengthened. In a letter to Halleck in Washington he described them as ". . . well-disciplined and hardy men who know no defeat and are not willing to learn what it is."

First thing next morning they pushed on into Port Gibson to find the bridges over the Bayou Pierre undefended but destroyed. A makeshift bridge was hurriedly constructed and the troops advanced a further eight miles that day. They were heading northeastward, away from the Mississippi, threatening to cut off the Confederate garrison at Grand Gulf, which promptly pulled out and hurried north toward Vicksburg. Porter's ships took over Grand Gulf.

On 3 May Grant ordered McClernand to maintain the push northeastward. Grant himself rode to Grand Gulf to find his headquarters and send messages to Washington: "I had not been with my baggage since the 27th of April and consequently had had no change of underclothing, no meal except such as I could pick up sometimes at other headquarters, and no tent to cover me. The first thing I did was to get a bath, borrow some fresh underclothing from one of the naval officers and get a good meal on the flagship. Then I wrote letters to the general-in-chief informing him of our present position . . ." Grant told Halleck: "This army is in the finest health and spirits. Since leaving Milliken's

Bend they have marched as much by night as by day, through mud and rain, without tents or much other baggage, and on irregular rations, without complaint, and with less straggling than I have ever before witnessed."

At his headquarters Grant received news that forced a major change of plan. The intention all along, after securing Grand Gulf as a supply base, had been that he should order McClernand's corps south to link up with General Banks and take the Confederate stronghold at Port Hudson before the final move was made against Vicksburg. But Grant now heard that Banks was still campaigning far up the Red River in Louisiana and could not hope to be in the Port Hudson area before 10 May and then only with 15,000 men. In his present buoyant mood, Grant could not accept such a delay: "I therefore determined," he wrote later, "to move independently of Banks, cut loose from my base, destroy the rebel force in rear of Vicksburg and invest or capture the city." It was the vital decision of the campaign and a highly controversial one.

Grant knew that Halleck, his military chief in Washington, would not approve of such defiance of the West Point rule book on strategy, but he also knew that messages took many days to pass between his headquarters and Washington. More to the immediate point, Grant also knew that his trusted right-hand man, General Sherman, now hurrying to join him, would disapprove strongly. He was right about that. Sherman traveled fast down the road from Milliken's Bend, painfully aware of its length and vulnerability, the impossibility of protecting it at all points. As soon as he arrived on the scene he sent a peremptory note to Grant: "Stop all troops until your army is partially supplied with wagons, and then act as quickly as possible, for this road will be jammed as sure as life if you attempt to supply 50,000 men by one single road." Grant replied: "I do not calculate upon the possibility of supplying the army with full rations from Grand Gulf. I know it will be impossible without constructing additional roads. What I do expect, however, is to get up what rations of hard bread, coffee and salt we can and make the country furnish the balance."

▲ *Ashore at last on firm dry ground to the south of Vicksburg, Grant ordered his vanguard to move rapidly toward Port Gibson. The Confederates retreated. The march on Vicksburg had started.*

▼ *Men of McClernand's army corps in the sharp but brief battle that took place before the Confederates left Port Gibson.*

LIVING OFF THE LAND

Grant was on his own now. He would manage without any help from Banks. He had dealt with McClernand's takeover bid. And he was virtually out of contact with his chiefs in Washington. It was his show.

Things were very different on the Confederate side of the hill. In late November 1862 President Jefferson Davis had put General Jo Johnston in overall charge of all their forces in the western sector. Davis toured the region in December, stressing to Johnston the key importance of holding Vicksburg. Johnston said he could do it but he needed a further 20,000 men. The reinforcements did not arrive. Jo Johnston was a man seriously out of sorts at this time. He had never fully recovered from the wounds received at the Battle of Seven Pines. He was frequently too sick to work. And he believed that the command he had been given was unmanageable, that his main armies – one in Tennessee, the other in Mississippi – were too far apart to give each other effective support in a crisis. He did not trust Jefferson Davis and had no high regard for his commander in the Vicksburg area, Pemberton.

It was fortunate for Grant that he found himself facing an enemy that was split both physically and psychologically. By 3 May Grant had more than 20,000 men on the east side of the Mississippi and more on the way, but he knew he was outnumbered by the Confederates. Pemberton, he reckoned, had some 25,000 troops in and around Vicksburg, and there were several thousand more in the Jackson area. He had to get between them, smash their communications, keep them guessing about his next moves, and do it all fast.

His dispatches at this time reveal his obsession with speed. On 3 May he wrote to Sherman: "It is unnecessary for me to remind you of the overwhelming importance of celerity in your movements." He told the Commissary at Grand Gulf: "There must be no delay on account of either energy or formality." They were ordered to load up ". . . regardless of requisitions or provision returns." He told an officer on his staff: "See that the Commissary loads all the wagons . . . Issue any order in my name that may be necessary to secure the greatest promptness in this respect . . . Every day's delay is worth two thousand men to the enemy." He was interested in every relevant detail. On 6 May he was urging the quartermasters at Grand Gulf to ". . . rush forward rations with all dispatch . . . How many teams have been loaded with rations and sent forward? I want to know as near as possible how we stand in every particular for supplies. How many wagons have you ferried over the river? How many are still to bring over? What teams have gone back for rations?"

The troops at the front were sent off in all directions to commandeer every wheeled vehicle and draft animal they could find. They came back with horses and mules and oxen, classy carriages and farm carts, anything that would help to carry ammunition and rations forward on the great adventure. They foraged for food as well and found that there was plenty of it. In his *Memoirs* Grant recalled: "Beef, mutton, poultry and forage were found in abundance. Quite a quantity of bacon and molasses were also secured from the country, but bread and coffee could not be obtained in quantity sufficient for all the men. Every plantation, however, had a run of stone, propelled by mule power, to grind corn for the owners and their slaves. All these were kept running while we were stopping, day and night, and when we were marching, during the night, at all plantations covered by the troops."

While waiting for Sherman's corps to reach them, Grant sent out strong reconnaissance parties from the other two corps to cross the Big Black River at Hankinson's Ferry and convince Pemberton that he now meant to march direct to Vicksburg. This was the obvious next move. But Grant knew

▼ *Confederate infantrymen. Left to right: a first lieutenant of the South Carolina Rifles; a private soldier; and a sergeant of the 4th Kentucky Regiment, with Vicksburg on his regimental Color. (Ron Volstad)*

that if he did that, Pemberton would be able to mass his entire force, in good defensive positions, along the broken country south of Vicksburg and he, Grant, would be forced to attack an enemy who probably outnumbered him and who certainly knew the ground better than he did. The fate of his army and the outcome of his long campaign would hang on one battle. Grant had a cleverer idea, one that might take a little longer but which would be much cheaper in lives and more certain of success. He would march east toward Jackson, where the enemy were much fewer in number, and cut the railroad link between Pemberton and Johnston. Once again, speed was of the essence.

Fast Marching

On the night of 6 May McPherson pulled his forward brigades back across the Big Black River and first thing next morning marched east to Willow Springs, where he joined McClernand's army corps. On the 7th McClernand pushed on toward Utica while Sherman marched from the Grand Gulf area to Hankinson's Ferry. On the 8th McPherson closed up behind McClernand. So it went on, the whole army progressing in rapid but controlled steps, each corps getting time to rest but always being close enough to the others for contact to be maintained and help given if needed.

Grant swung two of the corps – McClernand's and Sherman's – northward, the further to baffle Pemberton. Was he now rounding on Vicksburg? Or aiming to cut the railroad link between Vicksburg and Jackson? In fact, he was still heading for Jackson itself. In the early afternoon of 12 May McPherson's leading division, pushing along the main road eastward and only two miles short of Raymond, came under fire. A Confederate brigade with two batteries was blocking their advance. Major General John A. Logan, a prominent politician who was now proving to be a very able fighting commander, was with his leading brigade. He sent a message back asking for prompt support, deployed his men into position and attacked with vigor. The Confederates fled. Logan lost 66 killed and 339 wounded in the brief but fierce encounter; while the Confederates lost 100 men killed, 305 wounded and 415 taken prisoner.

As soon as Grant received the news of this little victory, he made another decision. Up to this point he had had troops stationed at the crossings of the Big Black River to prevent the Confederates getting behind him and smashing his communications with Grand Gulf. From now on he was not going to worry about this. The defenders of the crossing points were ordered to rejoin their divisions. If the Confederates wanted to waste their time looking for lines of communication and supply to destroy, they were more than welcome – if they could find them. Just before sailing off into the blue, Grant dispatched one final message to Halleck in Washington: "As I shall communicate with Grand Gulf no more, except it becomes necessary to send a train with heavy escort, you may not hear from me again for several days." He knew that the conservative Halleck would disapprove of his move, but he also knew that Halleck's inevitable order countermanding any such move, could not possibly reach him until the whole thing was done.

On the Confederate side the confusion was mounting. On 9 May President Davis had ordered Jo Johnston to get himself to Mississippi quickly and take over operational command. Johnston, complaining that he was really too ill, reached the state capital, Jackson, on the evening of 13 May to find that earlier that same day the Federals had cut the direct railroad link with Vicksburg. He sent a telegraph message to Richmond: "I am too late." He had only 6,000 troops to defend Jackson from the attack in overwhelming numbers that would surely come the following day.

General Pemberton, meanwhile, was trying to reconcile conflicting orders. President Davis had told him to hold Vicksburg at all costs. Now Johnston was telling him to muster all his available forces and confront Grant's army. This was probably the right strategy but not so easy to implement. Virtually without cavalry, Pemberton was finding it impossible to obtain firm information about Grant's movements and he was perplexed that Grant's supply lines could not be located. Furthermore, he had an uneasy feeling that if he pulled all his men out of Vicksburg, Grant might give him the slip and take the city. If that happened, it would be very hard – with supplies and reinforcements pouring down the river to sustain Grant's hold on the city – to prise him out again. So Pemberton compromised, left a strong garrison in Vicksburg and moved about with the rest of his army on the northern side of the Big Black River, too far away from the next action to have any influence on it.

By nightfall on 13 May, as Jo Johnston arrived in Jackson, Grant had his forces in position for the next day's attack. Sherman's army corps was camped at Raymond. McPherson's was a few miles northeast at Clinton on the railroad line. McClernand's corps was behind them, covering the rear. It rained heavily during the night and most of the men were sleeping in the open. It was still raining at daybreak when the two corps set off eastward on the roads that converged on Jackson. Stretches of the roads were under a foot or so of water but they pressed on and by 11 a.m. both corps were deployed for the attack.

The fight that followed was fierce but brief. On both fronts, the initial assaults were held. Grant, who was with Sherman on the right of the line, suggested that a strong unit be sent to probe the Confederate defenses farther round to the right. This was done and it was found that there were no defenses at all. Johnston, seeing that his troops had been turned, ordered a rapid retreat northward. Seventeen Confederate guns fell into Grant's hands and Jackson was his. McPherson had lost 37 men killed and 228 wounded. Sherman had only four killed and 21 wounded.

The day's action had been closely watched by Grant's son Fred, who had been in close attendance on the army's march inland from the Mississippi. He later recalled an incident as they were advancing toward Jackson that morning: "While passing through a piece of dense woods on the way, the enemy's sharpshooters opened fire on us. One of the staff shouted to my father that they were aiming at him. His answer was to turn his horse and dash into the woods in the direction whence the bullets were coming." Fred was among the first to reach the

▼ *The men of McPherson's 7th Division make the charge that broke the Confederate defenses at Jackson. Colonel Holmes's 2nd Brigade lost 30 men killed in this attack.*

The Advance to Vicksburg

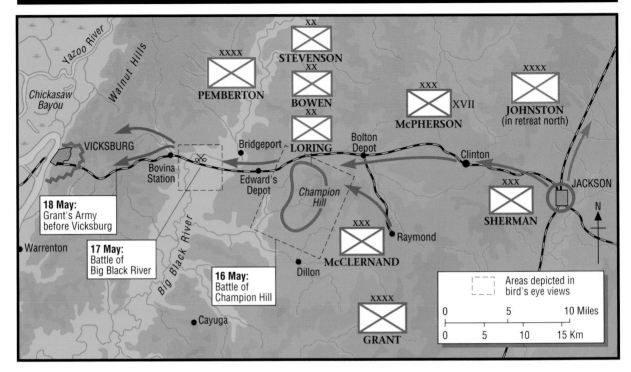

center of Jackson: "At this time I saw a mounted officer with a Union flag advancing toward the Capitol. I followed him into the building and entered the Governor's room, which had been hastily abandoned. Returning to the street, I saw the officer in the act of raising the Union flag over the building. Father and his staff, advancing at the head of the army, soon reached the State House, where I joined them, and went with them to the Bowen House, the best hotel in Jackson, where we took the room in which General Joseph E. Johnston had slept the night before."

For a while Jackson suffered a period of destructive anarchy. There were many Confederate stragglers and deserters at large, some runaway Negro slaves, and men from the Federal forces who were determined to celebrate their success with looting and rowdyism. Convicts escaped from the city jail and they joined in. Grant organized patrols to restore order. Then, on the morning of 15 May Grant ordered Sherman to destroy the city, it being a railroad and manufacturing center for *matériel*. Sherman, a thorough man, ". . . did the work most effectually," as Grant put it. A few weeks later, in July, Jo Johnston was once again in Jackson and

Sherman was besieging it. When Johnston slipped away overnight, Sherman moved in and set fire to most of what was left. So many buildings were destroyed that the city was wryly called "Chimneyville" because of the innumerable brick chimneys sticking up from the charred ruins.

▶ *Sherman's men enjoyed the task of rendering Jackson useless as a rail center.*

▶ *Far right: The fires started by Sherman's men were still blazing in Jackson when the Confederate soldiers marched back into the city. There was a rapturous reception; but only a few weeks later they marched out again as Sherman's army corps approached from the west to complete their devastation of the city.*

THE BATTLE OF CHAMPION HILL

Now, at last, Grant turned to head straight for Vicksburg, 35 miles to the west. His first objective had been achieved – he had put his army between Johnston and Pemberton. Grant's men were full of confidence, beginning to realize that this was a remarkable campaign. One gunner wrote: "If there ever was a jubilant army, Grant's army in Jackson was that night." But Grant allowed little time for celebration. He had the Confederates split and reeling, but he knew that they had reinforcements hurrying from the east and he meant to complete the job before they could intervene. He was helped in this by another bit of luck. A Federal spy, traveling in Confederate gray, brought him a copy of a message from Johnston ordering Pemberton to meet him, with all the force at his command, on the railroad line between Vicksburg and Jackson. Grant acted to spoil this move immediately. The morning after the taking of Jackson two of his army corps were on the march again – McPherson's to the Clinton area, McClernand's six miles farther west. Sherman's

corps stayed behind, briefly, to complete the destruction of Jackson as a military base.

Pemberton had been casting about south of the Big Black River, hoping to catch Grant in the rear. Now he received Johnston's summons to a meeting on the railroad and turned north. On the morning of 16 May his leading units made contact with Grant's vanguard to the east of Edwards Station. Pemberton deployed his troops in defensive positions on the slopes of a rough and wooded eminence called Champion Hill, which commanded the direct road to Vicksburg.

Grant was advancing westward along the line of the railroad and immediately south of it, with McPherson's corps on his right, McClernand's on the left, and Sherman's coming up quickly behind them. His forces totaled about 29,000 men, tough and fit and buoyant. In a sense, this was the moment Pemberton had been waiting for, the confrontation with Grant's army, but he was considerably outnumbered, having left more than 10,000 men behind to

An artist's impression of one of the actions in the Battle of Champion's Hill. John Logan leads his men into the attack.

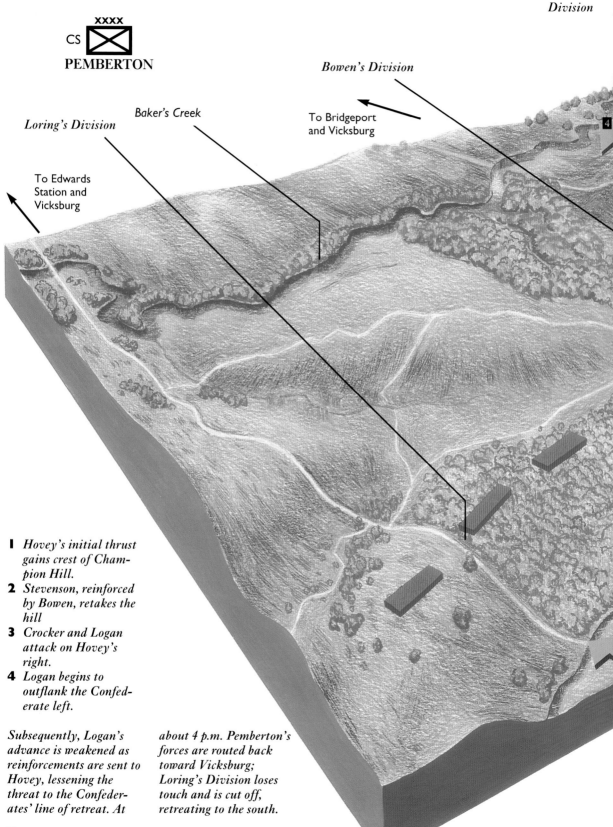

Stevenson's Division

CS ⊠ *XXXX*
PEMBERTON

Bowen's Division

Loring's Division

Baker's Creek

To Bridgeport
and Vicksburg

To Edwards
Station and
Vicksburg

4

1 *Hovey's initial thrust gains crest of Champion Hill.*
2 *Stevenson, reinforced by Bowen, retakes the hill*
3 *Crocker and Logan attack on Hovey's right.*
4 *Logan begins to outflank the Confederate left.*

Subsequently, Logan's advance is weakened as reinforcements are sent to Hovey, lessening the threat to the Confederates' line of retreat. At
about 4 p.m. Pemberton's forces are routed back toward Vicksburg; Loring's Division loses touch and is cut off, retreating to the south.

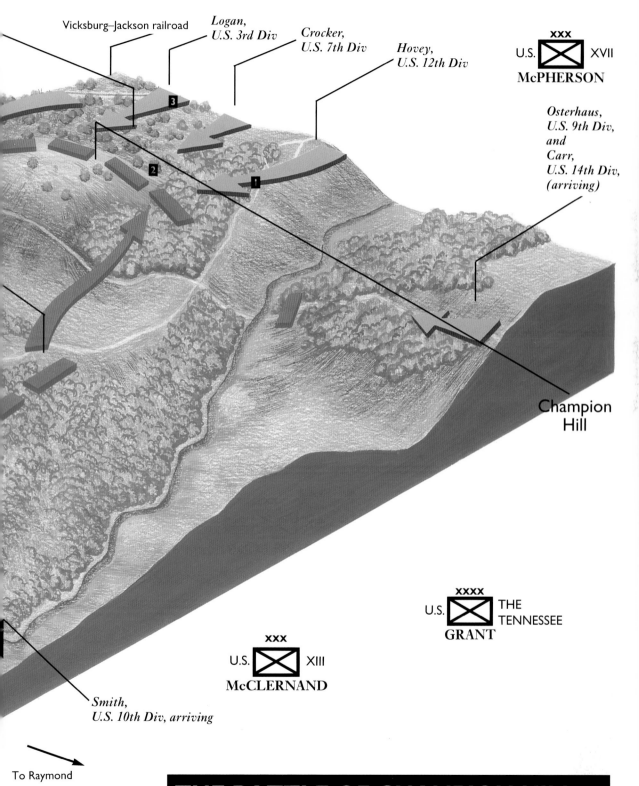

Vicksburg–Jackson railroad

Logan, U.S. 3rd Div

Crocker, U.S. 7th Div

Hovey, U.S. 12th Div

U.S. **McPHERSON** XVII

Osterhaus, U.S. 9th Div, and Carr, U.S. 14th Div, (arriving)

Champion Hill

U.S. **GRANT** THE TENNESSEE

U.S. **McCLERNAND** XIII

Smith, U.S. 10th Div, arriving

To Raymond

THE BATTLE OF CHAMPION HILL

16 May 1863, as seen from the southeast

protect Vicksburg. He had slightly fewer than 22,000 men on Champion Hill, many of them weary from days of ineffectual marching and counter-marching.

But the place Pemberton had chosen to make his stand was a good one. The summit plateau of Champion Hill stands some 140 feet above the surrounding countryside, commanding a wide prospect in all directions. It is rough ground, split by many gullies and steep-sided ravines, much of it thickly vegetated. It was difficult for the Federal troops to see exactly where the enemy's guns were, impossible to assess the strength of his defenses. The battle of Champion Hill was comparatively short, but because of the nature of the terrain it was confused and messy, decided in the end not by any brilliant stroke of generalship but by sheer weight of numbers. It was the fiercest and bloodiest engagement of the whole Vicksburg campaign.

The first Federal troops to come under fire were men of the 12th Division of McClernand's corps who, for some reason, were marching ahead of McPherson's army corps on the right of the line. The division was commanded by Brigadier General Alvin P. Hovey, an Indiana lawyer before the war and now an experienced and capable commander. He quickly deployed his regiments into line about a mile to the west of Bolton Depot and launched an uphill attack.

There was some initial success. They advanced about 600 yards and men of the 24th Iowa Brigade seized an enemy battery and took prisoners after a bayonet charge. Moments later, though, the Confederates countercharged and drove them back down the slopes again. A vicious, to-and-fro dogfight ensued in which Hovey became very hard-pressed.

McPherson's corps was close behind and John Logan's division moved into line on Hovey's right. Grant himself was soon on the scene and he got Logan to send a brigade to help Hovey. Another division, that of Brigadier General Marcellus M. Crocker, a sickly man but full of fight, soon joined in. By coincidence, it was these two divisional commanders, John Logan and Marcellus Crocker, who had been most actively involved in the fight for Raymond only four days earlier. Grant thought highly of both of them: "I regarded Logan and Crocker as being as competent division commanders as could be found in or out of the army and both equal to a much higher command. Crocker, however, was dying of consumption when he volunteered. His weak condition never put him on the sick report when there was a battle in prospect, as long as he

◄ *General James B. McPherson, the able commander of Grant's XVII Army Corps, in conference with two of his engineer officers.*

could keep on his feet. He died not long after the close of the rebellion."

The battle proper began at about midday and went on for almost four hours. The most intense fighting was concentrated at the northern end of the line where Hovey and Crocker were bearing the brunt. As Crocker's division moved into the front line, Logan pushed farther round to the west in an attempt to outflank the Confederate line. Grant, with his staff, had joined Logan and for a short time in the early afternoon, although they did not realize it, they had Pemberton virtually trapped. Grant described it in his *Memoirs*: "I found him [Logan] near the road leading down to Baker's Creek . . . Neither Logan nor I knew that we had cut off the retreat of the enemy. Just at this juncture a messenger came from Hovey, asking for more reinforcements. There were none to spare. I then gave an order to move McPherson's command by the left flank around to Hovey. This uncovered the rebel line of retreat, which was soon taken advantage of by the enemy."

Hovey, with active support from men of Logan's and Crocker's divisions, had been launching repeated attacks on the Confederate defenses, which were also under heavy, enfilading bombardment from two of McPherson's batteries to the north. Just before 4 p.m. the defense collapsed and the Confederates' retreat soon turned into a chaotic rout. Pemberton said: "We lost a large amount of artillery. The army was much demoralized; many regiments behaved badly." Colonel Edward Goodwin of the 35th Alabama Regiment described the scene in these words: "At this time our friends gave way and came rushing to the rear panic-stricken. I brought my regiment to the charge bayonets, but even this could not check them in their flight. The colors of three regiments passed through . . . We collared them, begged them, and abused them in vain." Colonel Goodwin was in Pemberton's First Division, commanded by Major General W. W. Loring, which completely lost touch with Pemberton's force in the retreat and took no further part in the Vicksburg campaign.

Grant sent two divisions of McClernand's corps, neither of which had been involved in much of the fighting, in hot pursuit of the enemy. It was an undoubted victory for Grant and it left the way open for his march on Vicksburg, but he was far from satisfied with the results of the day's work. In the first place, as he soon realized, he had momentarily been in a position to surround and capture Pemberton's army and had failed to do so. It would have meant a much longer and costlier fight on Champion Hill but would have spared him the long weeks of the siege of Vicksburg. In Grant's view no victory was complete if it did not involve the destruction of the enemy's army. Secondly, Grant was very far from pleased with the conduct of that persistent thorn in his side, Major General John A. McClernand.

Of his total force of nearly 30,000 men, Grant had only managed to get about half into the actual fighting. Although it was at the front, in the central and southern sectors, McClernand's army corps was remarkable chiefly for its inactivity – except for Hovey's division. It was not for want of asking. In his *Memoirs* Grant wrote: "McClernand, with two divisions, was within a few miles of the battlefield long before noon, and in easy hearing. I sent him repeated orders by staff officers fully competent to explain to him the situation. These traversed the wood separating us, without escort, and directed him to push forward; but he did not come."

According to Grant, McClernand not only made no effort to get into the thick of the fight, he actually sent orders to Hovey to pull out of it and rejoin his corps. Grant told Hovey to stay where he was. Hovey lost one-third of his division in the fight – 108 men killed, 365 wounded, 93 missing. He called Champions Hill "a hill of death" and said, "I never saw fighting like this." The total Federal losses were 410 killed, 1,844 wounded and 187 missing.

Things were much worse for Pemberton, however. He had lost 3,800 men altogether and 27 guns. And his army was badly shaken.

Big Black River

The pursuit of the fleeing Confederates was maintained until after nightfall, by which time they were across the Big Black River, some seven miles west of Champion Hill. Vicksburg was now little more than 20 miles away and Grant, ever impatient, got his men moving before 4 o'clock next morning. In the vanguard was Brigadier General Eugene A. Carr's division of McClernand's corps, and they soon came

LAWLER'S BRIGADE:
1 *23 Iowa*
2 *21 Iowa*
3 *11 Wisconsin*
4 *22 Iowa*

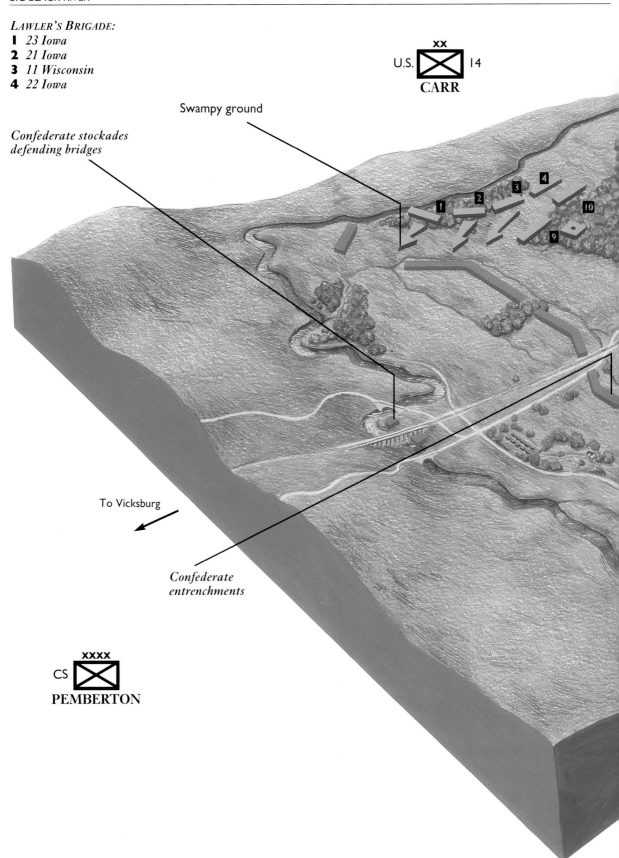

U.S. ⊠ 14
CARR

Swampy ground

Confederate stockades
defending bridges

To Vicksburg

Confederate
entrenchments

CS ⊠
PEMBERTON

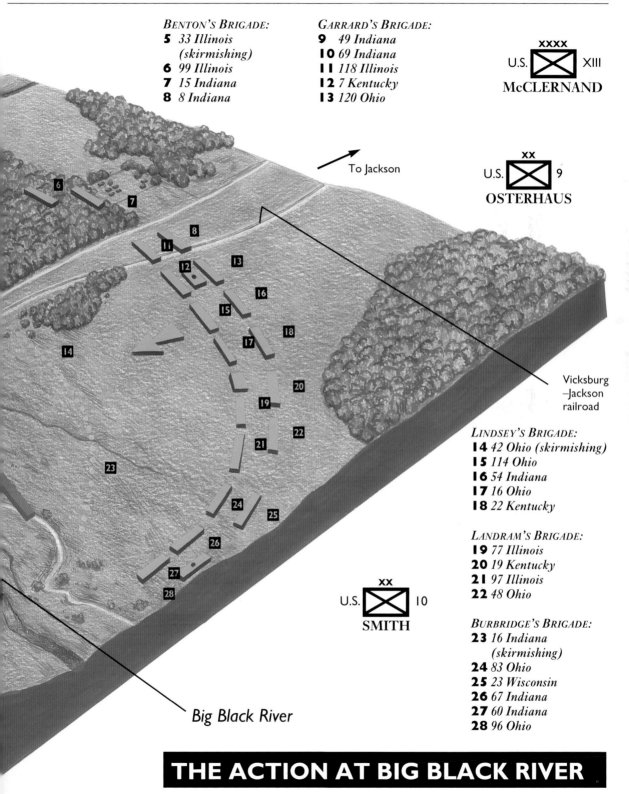

BENTON'S BRIGADE:
5 *33 Illinois (skirmishing)*
6 *99 Illinois*
7 *15 Indiana*
8 *8 Indiana*

GARRARD'S BRIGADE:
9 *49 Indiana*
10 *69 Indiana*
11 *118 Illinois*
12 *7 Kentucky*
13 *120 Ohio*

U.S. XIII
McCLERNAND

To Jackson

U.S. 9
OSTERHAUS

Vicksburg
–Jackson
railroad

LINDSEY'S BRIGADE:
14 *42 Ohio (skirmishing)*
15 *114 Ohio*
16 *54 Indiana*
17 *16 Ohio*
18 *22 Kentucky*

LANDRAM'S BRIGADE:
19 *77 Illinois*
20 *19 Kentucky*
21 *97 Illinois*
22 *48 Ohio*

BURBRIDGE'S BRIGADE:
23 *16 Indiana (skirmishing)*
24 *83 Ohio*
25 *23 Wisconsin*
26 *67 Indiana*
27 *60 Indiana*
28 *96 Ohio*

U.S. 10
SMITH

Big Black River

THE ACTION AT BIG BLACK RIVER

17 May 1863, as seen from the southwest, showing the Federal troop dispositions for the assault on the Confederate rearguard defensive line guarding the river crossings

◄ Their rapid advance involved Grant's men in a lot of improvised civil engineering, especially bridge building. McPherson's men are here depicted crossing the bridge they had hurriedly thrown across the Big Black River.

up against the Confederate force with eighteen guns that Pemberton had left to delay the advance and give him time to get the greater part of his army safely behind the Vicksburg defenses.

There were three bridges across the river close together at this point, two road bridges and one carrying the railroad line. The Confederate force was small, but they were holding a strong position from which they could fire on the Federal troops as they attacked across open and watery land. There was no doubt that in the end Grant's vastly superior numbers would prevail but he made careful dispositions for the attack, with McClernand's 9th Division, commanded by Brigadier General Peter J. Oster-haus, on the left, and the 14th Division, commanded by Brigadier General Eugene A. Carr, on the right. On the extreme right of the line was Carr's 2nd Brigade, led by a remarkable and unmistakable figure, Brigadier General Michael K. Lawler. His men were mostly from Iowa but he came from Illinois where he had been a farmer before the war. He was a very big man in all ways, so fat that he could not find a long enough swordbelt and had to hang his sword from a shoulder strap. But Grant said of him: "When it comes to just plain hard fighting I would rather trust old Mike Lawler than any of them."

In his *Memoirs* Grant described an odd incident which he said took place while he was completing his dispositions: ". . . an officer from Banks's staff came up and presented me with a letter from General Halleck, dated the 11th of May. It had been sent by the way of New Orleans to Banks to be forwarded to me. It ordered me to return to Grand Gulf and to cooperate from there with Banks against Port Hudson, and then to return with our forces to besiege Vicksburg. I told the officer that the order came too late, and that Halleck would not give it now if he knew our position. The bearer of the dispatch insisted that I ought to obey the order, and was giving arguments to support his position when I heard great cheering to the right of our line and, looking in that direction, saw Lawler in his shirt sleeves leading a charge upon the enemy. I immediately mounted my horse and rode in the direction of the charge, and saw no more of the officer who delivered the dispatch."

Grant of course was writing more than twenty years after the event, and was a dying man, so it is hardly surprising if he confused details. The only order dated 11 May from Halleck to Grant that can be found in the official records is nothing like as definite as Grant remembered. It merely states that ". . . if possible, the forces of yourself and of General Banks should be united between Vicksburg and Port Hudson so as to attack these places separately with combined forces."

It was General Lawler's impetuous charge, made before the order to attack had been given, that broke the Confederate resistance. The end of their defensive line was smashed, and the rest of the Federal line charged. The Confederates ran, set fire to the bridges and tried to escape. But the Federals took 1,700 prisoners and the eighteen guns. Lawler lost 27 men killed and 194 wounded. Grant immediately set his men to improvising new bridges. By now they were experienced at makeshift structural engineering and their bridges were ready by nightfall. Large bonfires were lit on the river bank and by their cheerful light, one by one, the regiments filed across. Grant sat on a log by the river, smoking cigars, and watching with quiet satisfaction as the last obstacle between him and the city of Vicksburg was crossed. His old comrade-in-arms, General Sherman, was with him.

Next morning, 18 May, McClernand and McPherson's army corps marched the last seven miles due west that brought them up against the Vicksburg fortifications. Sherman marched farther north to take possession, virtually unopposed, of the high ground north of the city – the heights he had failed to gain five months before in his attack on the Chickasaw Bluffs. The vital thing from Grant's

point of view was that this meant he could now reestablish a secure line of supply and communication, by means of Porter's boats on the Yazoo and Mississippi Rivers. In effect it also meant that there was no further danger of Johnston and Pemberton joining forces against him. For Grant's soldiers, it meant, too, that they could now look forward to plentiful supplies of bread and coffee. On the whole they had fed well on the march from Bruinsburg to the gates of Vicksburg, but they had missed their bread and coffee.

Grant went to see Sherman that same day. It was Sherman who had been most apprehensive about the idea of a long march through enemy country without a supply line of any kind. Now he apologized. He told Grant: "Until this moment, I never thought your expedition a success. I never could see the end clearly, until now. But this is a campaign; this is a success if we never take the town."

▼ *Grant's men approaching the eastern outskirts of the city of Vicksburg.*

THE SIEGE OF VICKSBURG

Around Vicksburg Pemberton's men had constructed a defensive line some seven miles in length. Pemberton reckoned that he had rations for 60 days. In addition to the civilian population of the city, he commanded more than 30,000 men. One of General McPherson's staff officers, when he first rode up the Jackson road and looked at the problem ahead, was impressed: "A long line of high, rugged, irregular bluffs, clearly cut against the sky, crowned with cannon which peered ominously from embrasures to the right and left as far as the eye could see. Lines of heavy rifle pits, surmounted with head logs, ran along the bluffs, connecting fort with fort and filled with veteran infantry . . . The approaches to this position were frightful – enough to appal the stoutest heart." Grant, too, thought the defenses looked formidable.

But Pemberton's army was trapped. For weeks now they had been out-generaled and out-fought. They had little confidence in their commander. Many of them were sick and even among those who were still fit, although they were experienced and tough and determined soldiers, there was a draining sense of fatalism, the feeling that it was only a matter of time before they would have to concede.

General Jo Johnston, 30 miles to the east and desperately trying to raise reinforcements so that he could threaten Grant's rear, thought the best thing now would be for Pemberton to fight his way out of

▼ *An artist's impression of the city of Vicksburg in the 1860s, as seen from the Mississippi.*

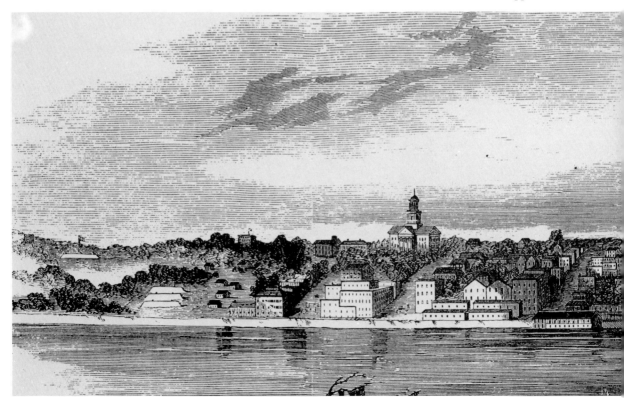

Vicksburg and link up with him and then together they could force Grant into battle before the Federal reinforcements came pouring in from the north. He wrote to Pemberton: "If it is not too late, evacuate Vicksburg and its dependencies, and march to the northeast." Pemberton discussed the matter with his generals and all agreed that their army lacked the spirit to attempt a breakout. Pemberton replied to Johnston: "I have determined to hold Vicksburg as long as possible."

Grant and his army, on the other hand, were in danger of overconfidence. After many days of hard marching and hard living, first in rain and mud and now in summer heat, they had tents and cooking utensils, full rations and an organized camp life. Their lines of supply and communication were secure again and before long the reinforcements would be arriving. They were beginning to think their general was invincible. And Vicksburg was surrounded. On the ground the Federal line stretched for fifteen miles from the Yazoo to the Mississippi, with Sherman in the north, McPherson holding the center, and McClernand in the south. The rivers were controlled by Admiral Porter's gunboats.

Grant reckoned that by now the Confederate troops would be seriously demoralized by their long retreat and their defeats at Champion Hill and the Big Black River, and he wanted to finish the job before Jo Johnston had time to get into the action. So in the early afternoon of 19 May – the day after he had arrived in front of Vicksburg – he launched an assault on the Confederate line. It was a failure. The Confederate troops may have been dispirited but they were well dug in. Their positions commanded wide angles of fire, and it was a comparatively simple matter to beat off the attack. Grant gained some ground here and there but at no point could his men break through the defensive line.

Initial Assaults

He spent the next two days preparing for a bigger and better-organized assault. On the morning of 22 May his guns opened up a tremendous bombardment, and at 10 o'clock the men of all three army corps attacked across the open ground. Grant later wrote: "The attack was gallant, and portions of each of the three corps succeeded in getting up to the very parapets of the enemy and in planting their

battle flags upon them; but at no place were we able to enter."

In the center of the line several of McPherson's regiments – from Iowa, Illinois and Wisconsin – scaled the walls of a Confederate fort by the railroad, seized it and succeeded in holding it for more than two hours despite repeated counterattacks. Then Texas units, with fixed bayonets, got among them and hurled them out. All along the line the fighting was furious. A colonel from Illinois spoke of, ". . . the most murderous fire I ever saw." Federal losses this day were 502 men killed, 2,550 wounded, 147 captured or missing.

At one point in the southern sector McClernand saw his men reach the Confederate line ahead and some of them were waving their banners in a triumphant manner. He assumed they had broken through and promptly sent word to Grant, asking for reinforcements and renewed efforts by the other two army corps. Grant was dubious but acceded to McClernand's requests. The result was costly and unprofitable, and Grant was very angry. Two days later he said: "General McClernand's dispatches misled me as to the real state of the facts, and caused much of this loss. He is entirely unfit for the position of corps commander, both on the march and on the battlefield. Looking after his corps gives me more labor and infinitely more uneasiness than all the remainder of my department." There can be little doubt that he was going to get rid of McClernand. He had the power to do so, a telegram from Edwin Stanton, the War Secretary in Washington, read: "General Grant has full and absolute authority to enforce his own commands, and to remove any person who, by ignorance, inaction or any other cause, interferes with or delays his operations." Grant was biding his time.

▼ *Grant's first unsuccessful attempt to break through the Confederate defenses and into the city.*

Siege Operations

The failure of the two assaults persuaded Grant that there was nothing for it but to settle down to a long siege. He consoled himself with the reflection that at least the failures had demonstrated to his soldiers that Vicksburg could not be quickly or cheaply won. Perhaps that thought would reconcile them to the hot, slow, slogging work of a siege. And by now it was getting very hot indeed. Many in the Confederacy had cheered themselves up with the notion that their summer heat would be altogether too much for the palefaced men of the north. Grant and his men now set themselves to show this was just another piece of wartime wishful thinking.

A complex system of deep and wide trenches had to be dug, approaching ever closer to the Confederate defenses. Gun sites had to be constructed and protected. It meant a great deal of labor and movement, with the ever present risk of being picked off by marksmen on the rising ground ahead. Later on, tunnels were dug deep underground in an endeavor to get beneath the enemy strongpoints and blow them up. It was heavy, dirty, sweaty work. It was engineers' work really, and Grant was short of trained engineers. But, as they had shown in the early days of the campaign, his midwesterners were hard and practical and resourceful men. One of their few engineering officers said: "Whether a battery was to be constructed by men who had never built one before, a sap-roller made by those who had never heard the name, or a ship's gun carriage to be built, it was done, and after a few trials well done . . . officers and men had to learn to be engineers while the siege was going on."

Grant was sure that Pemberton could not get out of Vicksburg and equally certain that Johnston would not want to get in. He told a staff officer: "If Johnston tries to cut his way in we will let him do it, and then see that he doesn't get out. You say he has 30,000 men with him? That will give us 30,000 more prisoners than we now have." Reinforcements were arriving almost daily, building up his army to more than 71,000 men, with 248 guns, six siege guns (32-pounders), and a battery of large-caliber naval guns, supplied by Admiral Porter and manned by sailors. In addition to manning the northern sector of the line facing Vicksburg, Sherman was given the job of

▲ *At first, the Federal troops made headway against the defenses; but these footholds were swept away by the Confederate counterattack.*

safeguarding the army's rear, and by late June something like a half of Grant's entire force was encamped to the east, awaiting the approach of Jo Johnston. During these weeks Grant was everywhere, studying the progress of his siege operations, encouraging his men, talking to them in his easy, unpretentious way. He told one group: "Pemberton is a Northern man who has got into bad company." More than once he was bawled at for casually exposing himself to sniper fire.

It was some time during this period of preparation that Grant is alleged to have fallen for his ancient tempter, the whiskey bottle. The tale was told, long after the war, by a correspondent for the *New York Herald* called Sylvanus Cadwallader, whose memoirs (not published until 1955) described

Grant's second attempt to seize the city – on 22 May 1863 – came closer to success than the first but was finally repulsed with serious losses on the Union side.

a visit Grant made to the Mississippi area which led to a two-day drinking session on one of the ships. There is no other evidence for this bender and it may be nothing more than the product of a newspaperman's imagination. Certainly, for most of the long campaign, the watchful and close attendance of John A. Rawlins, his chief of staff, precluded any alcoholic backsliding.

Naturally, rumors of Grant's excessive drinking continued to be circulated by his ill-wishers. President Lincoln had to listen to much of this talk and dealt with it in masterly fashion. Carl Sandburg, in his massive biography of the President, recounts a story Lincoln is said to have told one of his visitors. "One day a delegation headed by a distinguished doctor of divinity from New York, called on me and made the familiar complaint and protest against Grant's being retained in his command. After the clergyman had concluded his remarks, I asked if any others desired to add anything to what had already

▲ *Major General E. O. C. Ord, who took command of Grant's XIII Army Corps on 18 June 1863, the day McClernand was finally dismissed.*

▶ *The view from the extreme right of Grant's investing line, above the point at which the Mississippi makes an acute turn to flow below the city. This part of the line was held by Sherman's army corps.*

been said. They replied that they did not. Then looking as serious as I could, I said: 'Doctor, can you tell me where General Grant gets his liquor?' The doctor seemed quite nonplussed, but replied that he could not. I then said to him: 'I am very sorry, for if you could tell me I would direct the Chief Quartermaster of the army to lay in a large stock of the same kind of liquor, and would also direct him to furnish a supply to some of my other generals who have never yet won a victory.'"

Lincoln was delighted with Grant's progress and toward the end of May he wrote to a congressman: "Whether Gen. Grant shall not consummate the capture of Vicksburg, his campaign from the beginning of the month up to the 22nd day of it, is one of the most brilliant in the world."

It was toward the end of May, too, that McClernand made his fatal move. He issued an order to his army corps, congratulating them on their achievements and implying that if they had been given

proper support in the assault on 22 May, Vicksburg would have been theirs. A week or two later the order was printed in some Northern newspapers, presumably to enhance McClernand's image and political chances in Illinois. Both Sherman, who hated the press at the best of times, and McPherson protested to Grant. Grant asked McClernand for a copy of the order. McClernand complied and said he stood by what he had said. On 18 June Grant issued an order of his own: "Major General John A. McClernand is hereby relieved from the command of XIII Army Corps. He will proceed to any point he may select in the state of Illinois and report by Letter to Headquarters of the Army for orders." McClernand was replaced by the man who had been

his second in command, Major General E. O. C. Ord, a reliable if unremarkable commander.

Inside Vicksburg

For the Confederates trapped in Vicksburg these were increasingly terrible weeks. Grant's trench works crept closer all the time. His bombardment from all sides was relentless. Food became scarce and drinking water even more so. Many soldiers and civilians were sick and all were hungry. The soldiers took it with a resigned stoicism. Colonel Ashabel Smith of the 2nd Texas Regiment said: "Up to the last moment of siege the men bore [their hardships] with unrepining cheerfulness." After the surrender

◀ *Confederate lines at the rear of Vicksburg; from a contemporary photograph.*

◀ *The headquarters of the Union Signal Corps before Vicksburg.*

The Vicksburg Defenses

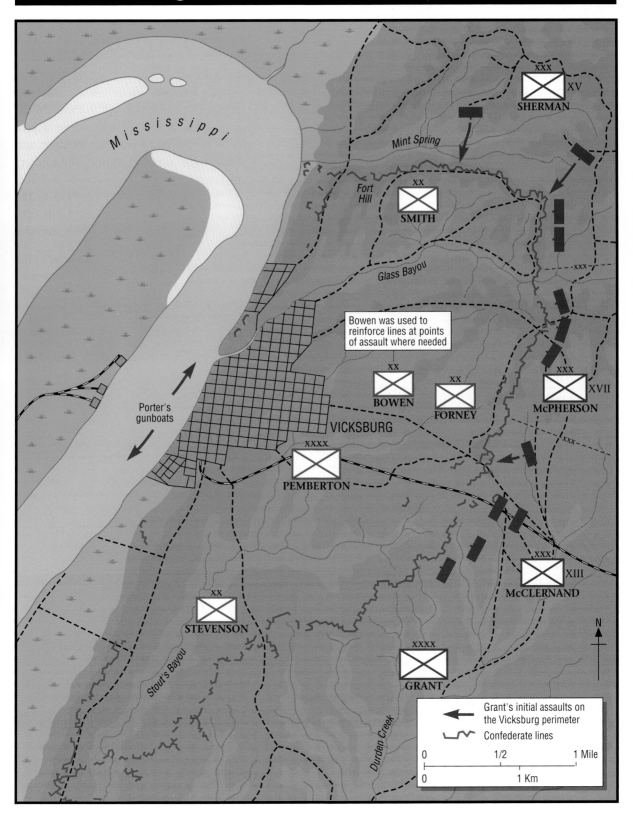

Mississippi

Mint Spring

Fort Hill

Glass Bayou

Bowen was used to reinforce lines at points of assault where needed

Porter's gunboats

VICKSBURG

Stout's Bayou

Durden Creek

XXX
SHERMAN
XV

XX
SMITH

XX
BOWEN

XX
FORNEY

XXX
McPHERSON
XVII

XXXX
PEMBERTON

XX
STEVENSON

XXXI
McCLERNAND
XIII

XXXX
GRANT

N

Grant's initial assaults on the Vicksburg perimeter

Confederate lines

0	1/2	1 Mile

0	1 Km

one of their generals said: "I have rarely heard a murmur of complaint. The tone has always been, '. . . this is pretty hard, but we can stand it.'" A journalist in the city later wrote: "By the middle of June, Vicksburg was in a deplorable condition. There was scarcely a building but what had been struck by the enemy's shells, while many of them were entirely demolished."

One of the soldiers noted in his diary: "The fighting is now carried on quite systematically . . . in the morning there seems to be time allowed for breakfast, when all at once the work of destruction is renewed. There is about an hour at noon and about the same at sunset. Taking these three intervals out, the work goes on just as regularly as on a well-regulated farm and the noise is not unlike the clearing up of new ground when much heavy timber is cut down." Emma Balfour, the wife of a Vicksburg doctor, also kept a diary in which she wrote: "As I sat at my window I saw mortars from the west pass entirely over the house, and the shells from the east passing by – crossing each other and this terrible fire

▲ *Part of McPherson's Corps in place before Vicksburg. It was in this sector of the lines that Pemberton and Grant were to meet.*
◄ *Logan's 3rd Division of McPherson's Corps showing the exploding of the mine under the Confederate fort near the Jackson road.*
▶ *Top right: An artist's dramatic impression of a railroad accident in the forests of Mississippi that did nothing to help General Johnston's efforts to get reinforcements. Below right: A funeral on the levee at the Duckport Canal.*

The view from General Hovey's divisional head-quarters at the southern end of the besieging line. A lithograph after a sketch made by A. E. Mathews.

▲ *An artist's impression of the view Grant's investing forces must have had of the city that had been their objective for so long. The imposing building in the center was the courthouse, built only five years earlier. The Confederates used the clocktower as a lookout point and signal station. Union gunners used it as a ranging point. The building survived the siege and is now a museum.*

◀ *Grant organized his siege lines very thoroughly. This was "Battery Hickenlooper," an important point close to the Jackson road.*

raging in the center . . . I see we are to have no rest." A merchant's wife took refuge in a cave and there gave birth to a son whom she called Siege.

Many civilians took to living in caves, carved out of the yellow clay hillsides. They were safe from the shelling there and some tried to make the caves homely with rugs and carpets, beds and chairs, but it was far from pleasant. One woman wrote: "It was living like plant roots. We were in hourly dread of snakes. The vines and thickets were full of them, and a large rattlesnake was found one morning under a mattress on which some of us had slept all night." Food supplies ran low. They made bread with corn and dried peas, in equal proportions. One soldier said: "It had the properties of indiarubber and was worse than leather to digest." The meat of horses, dogs and rats was available in the butchers' shops. By the beginning of July they were slaughtering their mules as well. Soldiers were subsisting on "one small biscuit and one or two mouthfuls of bacon per day."

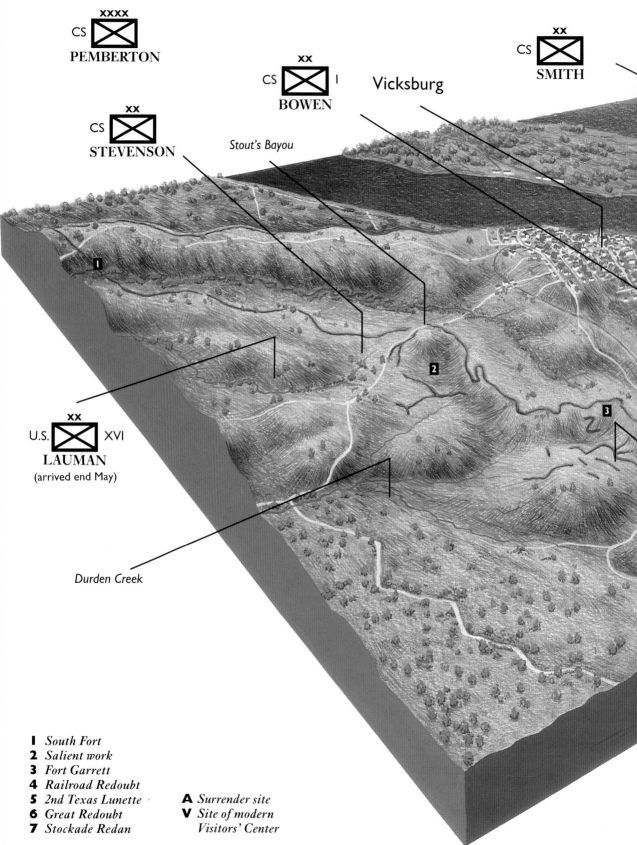

CS XXXX **PEMBERTON**

CS XX I **BOWEN**

CS XX **STEVENSON**

CS XX **SMITH**

Vicksburg

Stout's Bayou

1

2

3

U.S. XX **XVI** **LAUMAN** (arrived end May)

Durden Creek

1 *South Fort*
2 *Salient work*
3 *Fort Garrett*
4 *Railroad Redoubt*
5 *2nd Texas Lunette*
6 *Great Redoubt*
7 *Stockade Redan*

A *Surrender site*
V *Site of modern Visitors' Center*

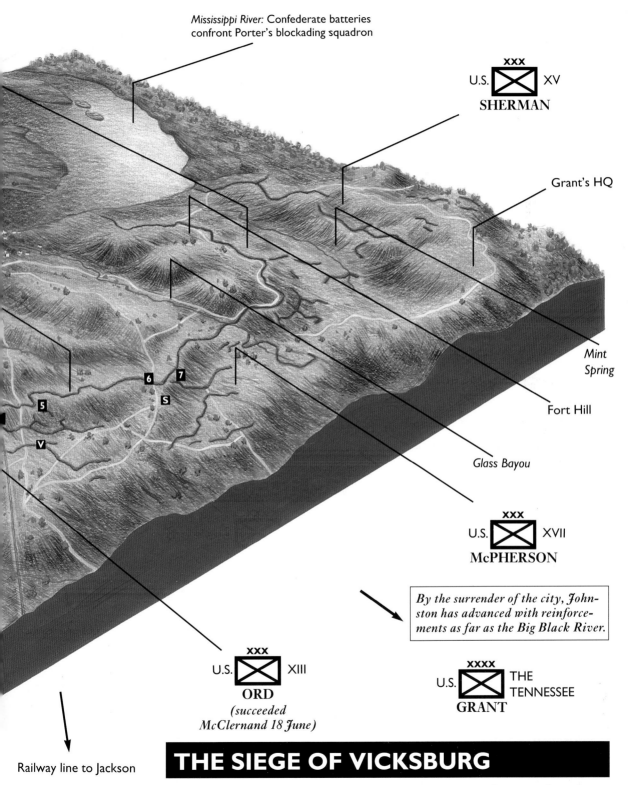

Mississippi River: Confederate batteries confront Porter's blockading squadron

U.S. XXX XV
SHERMAN

Grant's HQ

Mint Spring

Fort Hill

Glass Bayou

U.S. XXX XVII
McPHERSON

By the surrender of the city, Johnston has advanced with reinforcements as far as the Big Black River.

U.S. XXX XIII
ORD
(succeeded McClernand 18 June)

U.S. XXXX THE TENNESSEE
GRANT

Railway line to Jackson

THE SIEGE OF VICKSBURG

End May to 4 July 1863, as seen from the southeast, showing the siege works as fully developed

◄ *McPherson's engineers worked hard to destroy a key point in the center of the Confederates' defenses, the fort above the main Vicksburg to Jackson road. The idea was to mine under the fort, then blow it up. First they pushed trenches and parapets as close as they dared. Then an underground gallery was built. Soldiers who had been coal miners in civilian life were organized – in two shifts of eighteen men each – to dig the tunnel, shore it up, and remove the soil.*

◀ *Sherman's extreme right flank in the Union line before Vicksburg.*

▶ *The entrance to the gallery of the Union mine.*

▼ *Once directly under the fort, the Federal sappers planted 2,200 pounds of gunpowder, laid their fuses, and blew it up at 3 p.m. on 25 June.*

▲ *The fort was destroyed and Union troops poured into the crater that had been created. But they were pinned down there by fierce Confederate fire and had to pull back again.*

▼ *Men of Logan's Division pouring into the crater – and being carried out.*

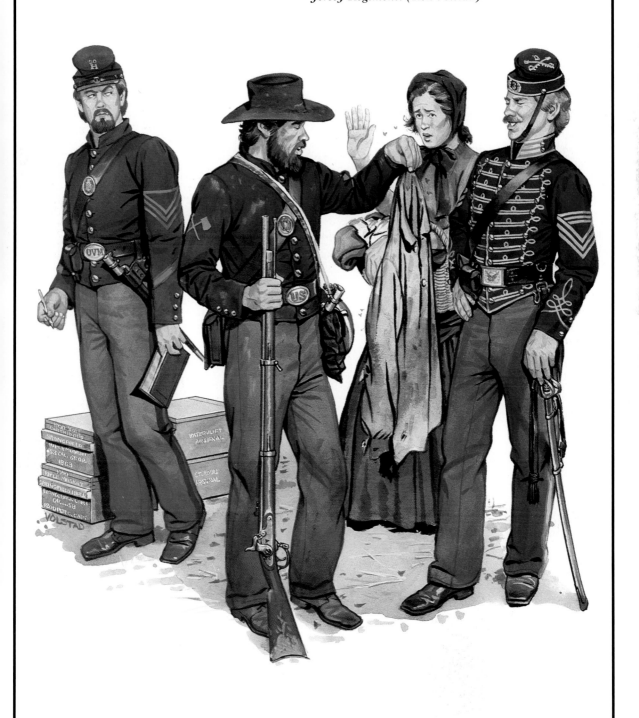

Uniforms of the Union army. Left to right: a company quartermaster sergeant of the 30th Ohio Volunteer Infantry Regiment; a pioneer of the 17th Illinois; and a Regimental quartermaster sergeant of the 3rd New Jersey Regiment. (Ron Volstad)

Pemberton grew increasingly pessimistic. One night he had the idea that his army might escape across the river to the Louisiana side, and started work on the building of crude craft. But Grant heard of this and alerted Admiral Porter who took immediate measures to prevent any escape that way.

The Confederates' best hope lay in the other direction. Jo Johnston had gathered an army of 32,000 men. By late June he was approaching Grant's lines from the south, planning to stage a diversionary attack that would give Pemberton a chance to fight his way out. Pemberton put the plan

◄ *Union headquarters, 3 July. Grant receives Pemberton's message proposing an armistice leading to the surrender of Vicksburg.*

◄ *Below left: an artist's impression of the first meeting of Generals Grant and Pemberton to discuss terms of surrender.*

► *Below right: Grant arrives at Pemberton's Vicksburg house on 4 July.*

to his generals and they were of the unanimous opinion that, although their men were still fit enough to man the defenses, none of them was in any shape for active campaigning in the field. Brigadier General Louis Herbert stated the case: "Forty-eight days and nights passed in the trenches, exposed to the burning sun during the day, the chilly air of night; subject to a murderous storm of balls, shells and war missiles of all kinds; cramped up in pits and holes not large enough to allow them to extend their limbs; laboring day and night; fed on reduced rations of the poorest kinds of food, yet always cheerful . . ." Johnston hoped to stage the diversion and the breakout on 6 July. But at 10 a.m. on the 3rd white flags began to appear along the Confederate lines. The firing died down and two Confederate officers rode out with a letter from General Pemberton to General Grant.

The Surrender

Pemberton's letter said that the Vicksburg garrison could hold out much longer, but that in the interests of preventing further suffering and loss of life, he proposed an armistice and the setting up of a com-

mission that would decide surrender terms. It was a ploy and Grant would have none of it. In his reply he said: "The useless effusion of blood you propose stopping by this course can be ended at any time you may choose, by the unconditional surrender of the city and garrison."

The two men came face to face at 3 o'clock that afternoon. They knew each other, they had served for a time in the same division during the Mexican War, but it was a frosty encounter. Pemberton was edgy and Grant was firm, but they finally agreed that Grant would send another letter that night stating his final terms.

That evening Grant had a meeting with his corps and divisional commanders, a meeting that he later described as, ". . . the nearest approach to a 'council of war' I ever held." The chief subject for discussion was whether or not they should offer to parole Pemberton's army, not send them to the prison camps of the north but to leave them in the Confederacy, having made them all sign promises to take no further part in the fighting. Some of them would break the promise, but it seemed likely that the great majority would not. They were mostly men from the southwestern states and could be

relied upon to take the first chance that came along to escape from the army and go back home. It seemed sensible to let the Confederacy have that problem rather than face the massive administrative task of shipping them all north and then looking after them for the duration. Finally they decided to offer parole and Grant sent his promised letter.

Pemberton accepted the new terms promptly and on the morning of 4 July John Logan marched his division into the city of Vicksburg and took control. Sherman was ordered to switch his whole attention to driving Jo Johnston out of the state of Mississippi and smashing Confederate communications to the east. He set about it immediately and with a will. Grant rode into Vicksburg, had a cool meeting with Pemberton and his generals, then went down to the riverside for a reunion with Admiral Porter.

The job was done at last. They took nearly 31,000 prisoners, 170 cannon and 60,000 rifles. In the whole campaign, from November 1862 to July 1863, they had put well over 40,000 Confederate soldiers out of active participation in the war. Grant himself had lost fewer than 10,000 men.

He now did all that he could to ensure that the defeated men were not abused or humiliated. In his first letter to Pemberton he had said: "Men who have shown so much endurance and courage as those now in Vicksburg, will always challenge the respect of an adversary and, I can assure you, will be treated with all the respect due to prisoners of war." In his *Memoirs* he recalled: "Our soldiers were no sooner inside the lines than the two armies began to fraternize. Our men had had full rations from the time the siege commenced, to the close. The enemy had been suffering, particularly toward the last. I myself saw our men taking bread from their haversacks, and giving it to the enemy they had so recently been engaged in starving out. It was accepted with avidity and with thanks."

▶ *Top right: an artist's impression of the scene, from the Confederate side, when the Federal army marched in to take charge of Vicksburg.*

▶ *Below far right: Logan's division enters*

Vicksburg by the Jackson road on 4 July.

▶ *Near right: Vicksburg Court House, which had been a landmark during the siege; from a photograph taken seventeen years later in 1880.*

THE CONSEQUENCES

Two coincidences made the news of Vicksburg's surrender particularly welcome in the North. The date had a powerful symbolic connotation. The Fourth of July was the day, as it still is, when Americans traditionally celebrated their achievement of independence from British colonial rule. Of greater practical importance was the fact that the victory at Vicksburg happened at the same time as the great and terrible victory at Gettysburg in southern Pennsylvania.

Only two months earlier things had looked blacker than ever for the North. The Confederate general-in-chief, Robert E. Lee, won his brilliant victory, very much against the odds, at Chancellorsville in Virginia at the beginning of May. In the middle of the month he set off on another bold march into Northern territory, hoping that it might force the recall of many of Grant's soldiers to the eastern sector and so take the pressure off Vicksburg. Lee's advance was finally halted, and reversed, in the battle at Gettysburg, fought over the first three days of July 1863, the greatest and bloodiest battle ever fought in North America. The Federals suffered 23,000 casualties. Lee lost one-third of his army and had no alternative but to turn for home.

Those few days were the turning point of the Civil War. The two Northern successes, east and west, made it clear that the North's vastly superior strength, in men and industry, would prevail in the end. There was no further danger of Britain recognizing and helping the Confederacy. Three of the eleven breakaway states, those west of the Mississippi, were virtually lost to the Southern cause. Only five days after the fall of Vicksburg, Port Hudson, the last Confederate strong point on the river, was surrendered. As usual, President Lincoln said it best: "The Father of Waters again goes unvexed to the sea." When the news from Vicksburg reached Washington, Gideon Welles, the Navy Secretary, hurried round to tell the President, and for once that most articulate of men was almost at a loss. "I cannot, in words," he said, "tell you my joy over this result. It is great, Mr. Welles, it is great!" To Grant, Lincoln wrote:

"My dear General,

"I do not remember that you and I ever met personally. I write this now as a grateful acknowledgement for the almost inestimable service you have done the country. I wish to say a word further. When you first reached the vicinity of Vicksburg, I thought you should do, what you finally did – march the troops across the neck, run the batteries with the transports, and thus go below; and I never had any faith, except a general hope that you knew better than I, that the Yazoo Pass expedition and the like, could succeed. When you got below, and took Port Gibson, Grand Gulf and vicinity, I thought you should go down the river and join Gen. Banks; and when you turned northward East of the Big Black, I feared it was a mistake. I now wish to make the personal acknowledgement that you were right, and I was wrong."

Ever since the beginning of the war Lincoln had been searching in vain for an effective military commander, a general-in-chief who would do for the North what Robert E. Lee was doing so ably for the South. Many were given the chance to prove themselves and all failed – through senility or incompetence, excessive caution or overconfidence, or sheer bad luck. Now Lincoln began to wonder whether the solution might lie in the eastern sector.

He took his time over the decision. In November 1863 Grant won another punishing victory, at Chattanooga. Early the following March he was summoned to Washington to be promoted to lieutenant general, the army's highest rank, which meant that he would be in charge of all the Federal armies. The appointment proved a wise one. It was Grant who, in April 1865, met Lee at Appomattox and accepted the final surrender of the Southern army. Three

▶ *Vicksburg from the north, after a sketch made subsequent to the surrender.*

▼ *The attack on Port Hudson, which surrendered to the Federal forces five days after the surrender of Vicksburg.*

years later Grant became President but that is another, and not so triumphant story.

The great innovation of the Vicksburg campaign was the discovery by Grant that a large army could operate deep in enemy territory without worrying about its supply lines, so long as it was in country rich enough in food production. Oddly, it was the man who had been most apprehensive about Grant's adventure when it started, General Sherman, who

put the lesson to its next and most cruelly effective use in his march through the Deep South in the winter of 1864–5.

The campaign saw another innovation that was to prove significant for the rest of the war, and indeed for the American armed services ever since – the employment of Negroes as fighting men. Lincoln's Emancipation Proclamation of 1 January 1863 had declared that all Negroes behind Confederate

lines were regarded as free by the Federal government. Until this time Lincoln's overriding war aim had been simply to restore the original United States. From this time on, the ending of Negro slavery was an equally important objective.

The next big issue in the North was whether or not Negroes should be enlisted in the fighting services. They had long been employed behind the lines, generally as laborers. Should they be given arms? The question was hotly debated. Grant made his view plain: "I have given the subject of arming the Negro my hearty support. This, with the emancipation of the Negro, is the heaviest blow yet given the Confederacy . . . By arming the Negro we have added a powerful ally. They will make good soldiers and taking them from the enemy weakens him in the same proportion as they strengthen us."

The new soldiers were given their first sizable test on 7 June 1863 at Milliken's Bend, on the Louisiana bank of the Mississippi above Vicksburg. By that time Grant's main army was besieging Vicksburg, but he had left small garrisons behind him at vital points and the force at Milliken's Bend was composed of white and Negro troops, though all the officers were white. They were attacked by 1,500 Texan Confederates and a fierce little battle, at very close quarters, ensued. The Confederates were driven off. In his *Memoirs* Grant wrote: "This was the first important engagement of the war in which colored troops were under fire. These men were very raw, having all been enlisted since the beginning of the siege, but they behaved well." By the end of the Civil War one-tenth of the Federal army was Negro, though there were very few black officers.

THE BATTLEFIELD TODAY

The U.S. National Park Service has an extensive National Military Park, set in rolling green parkland, at the northeastern edge of the city of Vicksburg. The Visitors' Center has many exhibits and an audiovisual program about the Vicksburg campaign and siege. Visitors who are prepared to walk a total of sixteen miles can inspect the sites of important events during the siege, Federal trenches and battery positions, Confederate earthworks and fortifications. The park also includes Vicksburg National

◀ *The arrival of* **Imperial** *at New Orleans, signifying that the whole length of the Mississippi now lay under Federal control and that the Confederacy was surrounded and split.*

▶ *The statue of Ulysses S. Grant in Vicksburg National Military Park.*

Cemetery with the graves of many of the Federal dead and also of men who were killed in the Spanish-American War, the two World Wars of this century and the Korean War.

Close to the cemetery is a museum displaying the U.S. gunboat *Cairo* which was sunk in the Yazoo River on 12 December 1862 while attacking Confederate batteries. Said to have been the first ship ever to be sunk by an electrically detonated mine, she was salvaged in the 1960s.

At Grand Gulf there is a Military Monument Park, displaying the cannon that successfully defended the port against Admiral Porter's attack on 29 April 1863. The State Historical Museum at Jackson has many exhibits relating to the city's Civil War experiences.

▲ *The Visitors' Center at Vicksburg National Military Park.*

CHRONOLOGY

1862 October: U. S. Grant given command of the Army of the Tennessee.

November: Grant marches south along the line of the Mississippi Central Railroad.

8 December: Sherman sent back to Memphis with orders to attack Vicksburg.

20 December: Earl Van Dorn's cavalry destroy Grant's supply depot at Holly Springs.

21 December: Grant begins retreat from Oxford.

26 December: Sherman lands his corps on the Yazoo banks above Vicksburg.

29 December: Sherman's attack on the Chickasaw Bluffs repulsed.

1863 January to March: Grant's army and Porter's navy try to force a series of different routes toward Vicksburg, north and west of the city.

March–April: McClernand marches his corps to the New Carthage area.

16–17 April: Porter's ships and transports run past the Vicksburg guns.

29 April: Porter's gunboats fail to silence the batteries at Grand Gulf.

30 April: McClernand's corps cross the river to Bruinsburg and take Port Gibson.

1–2 May: Confederates evacuate Grand Gulf. Porter's ships sail in.

9 May: Jefferson Davis sends Jo Johnston to take charge of the defense of Vicksburg.

12 May: Grant takes Raymond.

14 May: Grant takes Jackson.

16 May: Grant drives Pemberton's army off Champion Hill.

17 May: Grant drives Pemberton's men from the Big Black River crossing points.

18 May: Siege of Vicksburg begins.

19 May: Grant's first assault on the defenses is beaten back.

22 May: Second assault is beaten back.

18 June: Grant sacks McClernand and replaces him with Ord.

3 July: Pemberton asks for an armistice.

4 July: Grant's surrender terms are accepted and his army moves in to the city.

A GUIDE TO FURTHER READING

The key source is U. S. Grant's *Personal Memoirs*, vol. 1, first published in 1885. It gives a plain, readable, dynamic and modest account of his life with none of the boastfulness or pettiness or acrimony that characterize the memoirs of so many commanders.

The other basic, original source is volume 3 of *Battles and Leaders of the Civil War* (R. U. Johnson and C. C. Buel, 1884).

By far the fullest account is given in Edwin C. Bearss's *The Vicksburg Campaign* (1986).

Other very useful books include:

CATTON, Bruce. *Grant Moves South*, 1960
—*Never Call Retreat*, 1966
—*This Hallowed Ground*, 1957
SANDBURG, Carl. *Abraham Lincoln: The War Years*, vol. 2, 1936
SHERMAN, W. T. *Memoirs*, 1875
SWINTON, W. *Decisive Battles of the Civil War*, 1986
WOODWORTH, S. E. *Jefferson Davis and his Generals*, 1990

WARGAMING VICKSBURG

The operation to capture Vicksburg is well defined in its objective, geography and time-scale to provide the wargamer with a perfect setting for a limited campaign. There are many complexities to be considered but once resolved these will no doubt stimulate and challenge the gamers.

The terrain dictated very much how the campaign would proceed, but there were political considerations too. A direct assault by the Union forces across the Mississippi on Vicksburg was deemed to be too costly. Although Sherman and McPherson favored the plan, Grant did not wish to withdraw his forces to Memphis and then from there make an overland drive on Vicksburg lest the movement be misconstrued by the public as a retreat. Grant's actual plan to move down the Mississippi, cross to the east bank and then approach Vicksburg from the rear began in December 1862 and several attempts were made to reach Vicksburg. The best starting-point for a campaign would be 30 April 1863, because by then Grant had managed to find a crossing at Bruinsburg.

If the Confederate high command can be induced to cooperate they have every chance of defeating Grant. A large part of the problem was Johnston's pessimism and unwillingness to get a grip on the coordination of the widely dispersed forces at his command. He made no effort to hold the Federals at Jackson and failed to summon troops from Bragg in Tennessee. Furthermore, Pemberton's ineptitude for high command in diverting all of his cavalry after Grierson cost him, like Lee at Gettysburg, the "eyes of his army." But most of all Davis must take a full share of the blame for failing to realize the importance of the Mississippi and send troops from Holmes's army in Arkansas to Johnston at his request.

The Union side had command problems too. Their main problem was McClernand, the Illinois politician. Lincoln, a Republican, wanted to retain McClernand in the Union high command as encouragement for prowar Democrats. There was no love lost between this political general and his West Point colleagues. Sherman lost the battle of Chickasaw Bluffs through his desire to beat McClernand to Vicksburg. Although McClernand must have irritated Grant and the other corps commanders, in truth he was a capable commander, and was ultimately a victim of their jealousies. Grant was not above being petty himself and his continued and sometimes unjustified criticism may have led McClernand to seek recognition by releasing to the newspapers an address to his corps glorifying their achievements and playing down the other troops involved in the campaign – a mistake that gave Grant the opportunity he sought for McClernand's removal, since this not only contravened Grant's own but also the War Department's standing orders.

A multiplayer game may not be about which side wins, but how each general comes out of the campaign by comparison with his colleagues, in reference to his participation on the winning side. Campaign organizers may well give "brownie points" for individuals achieving self-glorification or fulfilling the self prophesies of the people they role-play.

Communications played a vital part in the campaign; the Mississippi River being the most important of them, essential to both sides and the reason for the campaign in the first place. The importance of the waterways in this area gives rise to naval operations. The presence of forts and batteries on the Mississippi and its tributaries made operations difficult for the Federals in bringing up supplies, but these were usually run past the Rebel batteries by night or protected by powerful gunboats.

Return fire from the Union boats against the batteries built on the high bluffs around Vicksburg was difficult. More successful in this operation were the "bombers," i.e., mortar boats which were specially constructed for this purpose. Shoals and obstructions in the river were real dangers and several Union vessels ran aground. Torpedoes (mines) were another danger in the rivers and several vessels fell victim to them. If spotted they could sometimes be detonated by smallarms fire.

Apart from reducing enemy batteries and escorting supply convoys, the Union gunboats were used in support of the army as at Haynes' Bluff, Arkansas Post and Milliken's Bend. A useful addition to the Mississippi Flotilla was Ellet's fleet of rams. These light craft were designed to ram enemy vessels and were unarmed, except sometimes for a couple of howitzers. Ellet made one of the first daylight runs past the Vicksburg batteries, but his vessel was captured. On the occasions that the main fleet made runs past Vicksburg, one out of six transports was sunk, with other vessels taking various damage too. The Confederates had but a handful of lightweight vessels during the campaign. Their best ship, *Arkansas*, had been scuppered on 6 August 1862, having caused the Union fleet much damage. The circumstances of her loss were unfortunate and avoidable. But for the impatience of Van Dorn *Arkansas* might well have been available in January 1863, which would have necessitated its destruction by Porter before Grant's campaign could go ahead.

Van Dorn did have the distinction of scuppering Grant's earliest plans, when his cavalry raided Grant's forward supply depot at Holly Springs. The brilliant Confederate cavalry leader Forrest also conducted a series of raids against Grant's communications to Tennessee. To divert the Confederate cavalry, Grant formed his own raiding column of 1,700 cavalrymen under Grierson which was entirely successful, covering the 600 miles from Grand Junction to Baton Rouge in fifteen days. Moving across land was as difficult as moving by water. Many of the roads were meandering quagmires; the map distance from Duckport to Hard Times was 28 miles, but in fact required a march of 64 miles. During the campaign the Federals carried three days' hardtack rations on standby, but wagon foraging parties operating fifteen miles from the roads were successful in providing forage for two months.

The actual siege operations for Vicksburg involve many features of wargaming that might best be played out on a large scale and with a detailed map depicting fortifications, sap heads, mining and countermining. These operations are time-consuming and would require an extended time-scale game period. The progress of field operations can be marked on the map, or perhaps a table could be laid out with a stand of figures representing a regiment or brigade. When it comes to transferring the action to the table top it will be necessary to build or buy ready-made items of siege warfare, i.e., breastworks, gun emplacements and abatis.

Also required will be some heavy artillery models. These are readily available in the popular wargame scales of 15mm and 25mm. They will be needed for the Confederate forts and batteries. Grant's siege train was inadequate from the start – six 32pdrs – and had to be supplemented by the navy's guns. During the siege the Confederates had better smallarms too because a large consignment of Enfields managed to get into the city. Many Rebels had a smoothbore loaded with buckshot in addition to a rifle-musket. Of course these arms were taken by the many Union regiments that had nothing better than converted smoothbores and Belgian rifles.

Union morale was good throughout the campaign. Confederate morale was poor after the defeat at Champions Hill, but recovered when the troops entered the Vicksburg defenses only to fall again in June when starvation had set in.

Finally the campaign can be tackled by stringing together its series of battles and perhaps allowing for military possibilities; for example, at Port Gibson, Pemberton might have been prepared for McClernand if his cavalry had been present. Johnston might have reinforced Gregg at Raymond and should have contested Jackson, allowing Pemberton a better chance of success at Clinton. The Confederate defense of the Big Black River was feeble; perhaps had they not been so demoralized by defeat at Champion Hill, they could have made the union assault costly.

Scenarios for the campaign can be found in the *Fire and Fury* scenario booklet (Champion Hill) and *Johnny Reb* rules scenario booklet *To the Sound of the Guns* (Vicksburg Assaults). Both are popular sets of rules, set at different command levels and both feature "what if?" game variations.